HINTS ON DRIVING.

HINTS ON

DRIVING

BY

CAPTAIN C. MORLEY KNIGHT

FOREWORD BY

MRS. NUBAR GULBENKIAN

ILLUSTRATED BY

G. H. A. WHITE

J. A. ALLEN & CO. LTD.
1 Lower Grosvenor Place, London S.W.1

British Library Cataloguing in Publication Data

Knight, C. Morley
  Hints on driving.
  1. Driving of horse-drawn vehicles
  I. Title
  798'.6   SF305

ISBN 0–85131–390–6

First published, July 1884.
Second Edition, revised, Dec., 1894.
Reprinted 1902
Reprinted 1905
Reprinted 1969
Reprinted 1973
Reprinted 1976
Reprinted 1979
Reprinted 1985
Reprinted 1988
Reprinted 1991

Printed and bound in Malta by
Interprint Ltd.

FOREWORD BY MRS. NUBAR GULBENKIAN

THIS excellent little book was written in an era when driving horses was not only a pleasurable pastime, but was almost the sole means of transport—hence, any hints on making driving more simple, and consequently, more safe, were of inestimable value.

This book should be considered the "British Driving Society's Bible"—for it contains wisdom for the tyro and also for the expert. The illustrations, especially those of the position of the hands and whip, should supply the answer to many arguments as to the *correct* way of holding reins and whip!

The chapters on harness are of very great interest, and should be carefully studied, particularly the fitting of collars—(so often in these days of second-hand harness, one sees ill-fitting collars, to the point where they can do permanent damage to a horse's windpipe). The coupling-reins in pair-horse driving are frequently wrongly adjusted. Capt. Morley-Knight explains and illustrates the adjustments of coupling-reins in the simplest manner, and these hints, if properly studied, should turn the tyro into an accomplished coachman, and cause the expert to become a really elegant whip! Above all, horses as well as their drivers will enjoy their outings much more, where horses are comfortable in their harness and drivers are competent to overcome any contretemps that may occur.

"Bonne promenade" to all!

M. B. Gulbenkian
1969.

CONTENTS.

CONTENTS

LIST OF ILLUSTRATIONS.

LIST OF ILLUSTRATIONS.

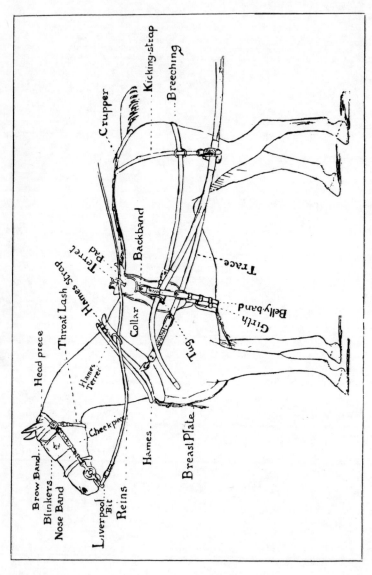

FIG. I.—SINGLE HARNESS ON HORSE.

HINTS ON DRIVING.

INTRODUCTION.

IN the following pages an attempt has been made to explain to beginners the rudimentary principles and niceties of driving.

In most treatises on this subject the minute details have been entirely omitted, the writer taking for granted that the reader has previously acquired some practical knowledge of harnessing and driving.

It is of course impossible to describe in a short essay every method of handling the ribbons, for well-known authorities even of the present day differ on so many points, that to discuss all would take too long. Nevertheless, as nothing has been considered too trifling to be explained, it is hoped that these hints may be especially useful to those who may not have been able to obtain any previous experience, and have not a thoroughly competent tutor at hand to teach them.

The difficulties which have to be overcome are so numerous that they cannot all be discussed in detail, for one of the greatest charms of driving consists in the ever-varying and complicated problems which are being constantly placed before the driver to solve— problems which must be solved at once without hesitation—and in no sport or pastime does the old saw, " He who hesitates is lost," more frequently prove true than in that of driving. Thus, though it happens that the same result may be obtained in a variety of ways by the practised hand, these notes being especially intended for the instruction of beginners, the author has endeavoured to solve, in the most simple and lucid manner, those problems only which are most likely to puzzle the novice.

After all, there is no way of learning to drive so instructive as sitting on the box-seat beside a first-class coachman, and carefully watching the movements of his hands. The novice is always tempted to confine his attention to the horses, and so omits to notice the manipulation of the reins at the critical moment. This omission on his part should be carefully avoided, as the crisis is over in so short a space of time that it is most important to keep the attention fixed almost entirely on the driver's hands, and carefully to commit to memory every detail of the handling of the ribbons. In this work no new theories on the art of driving have been advanced, but many very old ones have been specially emphasized by repetition—a course which has been considered justifiable on account of their great importance.

CHAPTER I.

HARNESS.

IT is often said by those who have little or no experience, that four horses steady themselves, and require therefore little skill in driving. This is a very great error, and a man who is keen to learn should make it his first aim to drive one horse well, and having thoroughly mastered this accomplishment, he should then proceed to handle a pair. In driving the great aim is to get the horses going well together, and all doing their fair share of work without taking more out of the driver than is absolutely necessary. In order to arrive at this it is essential to have the horses properly bitted, rightly coupled, comfortably poled up, and the harness fitted correctly.

To begin at the beginning, it is first of all necessary to see that the harness fits the horse. The collar is a very important point. This should lie flat on the horse's shoulders, so as to give sufficient room for the fingers to pass between it and the horse's neck at the sides, and the flat of the hand should be able to pass freely between the lower part of the collar and the horse's neck. Before putting the collar on, it ought to be widened by lateral pressure with the knee, so as not to hurt the horse's eyes while passing over his head. If the horse's shoulders should get rubbed, the best remedy is to apply plenty of sweet oil. This prevents the skin getting hard and the hair coming off. Salt water should never be used.

Fitting of harness. The collar.

Sore shoulders.

The hames should fit the groove in the Hames. collar, which should be well recessed, correctly all round and be buckled up tightly, otherwise in double harness they are very liable to be pulled out when going down hill, or when pulling up suddenly. To prevent this, a small strap may be buckled round the bottom of the collar over the hame links.

With a pair, the hames straps should be Hames buckled on so that the ends point inwards. straps.

The traces should be of such a length that The traces. the backband will lie on about the middle of the pad when the horse is in draught ; the horse will then not be drawing the cart by the backband. Care should be taken that the tugs are in front of the stops on the shaft, or a bad accident may occur owing to the cart running on to the horse's quarters.

The width of the reins may vary from The reins.

seven-eighths of an inch to an inch and a quarter, according to the length of the driver's fingers, but about one inch will be found the most suitable width for general purposes. The reins should not be too thick, or they will always be hard and stiff, while, on the other hand, if they are very thin, they will be uncomfortably soft in wet weather.

Backband.

In a two-wheeled cart the backband ought to be long enough to allow the shafts to hang level. There ought always to be a little weight on the shafts, as nothing looks so vulgar as shafts pointing up to the skies, with all the weight on the belly-band. It must be borne in mind that by letting down the shafts the balance of the cart can be very considerably altered. This alteration is often useful when there are four people in the cart, as few dog-carts balance well

Shafts and balance of cart.

with this number, the weight being nearly always on the belly-band. Few owners thoroughly appreciate what misery their friends undergo when made to occupy a back seat under these conditions, as they so rarely try it themselves.

The belly-band should not hang down Belly-band. quite loose, but, while allowing a little play of the shafts, should be tight enough to prevent them from tipping up to any extent.

The pad as well as the crupper should be Girth of pad. buckled up pretty tight if there are any steep hills to go down, and a breeching is not used ; otherwise the pad will slip forward and gall the horse's withers. Sore withers give a great deal of trouble and are difficult to cure. Another result of the pad slipping forward is chafing of the horse's elbows. On some horses the only way to prevent it is to fasten the girth back to the shaft on each side by means of straps. This plan is frequently used in hansoms in London. The pad itself should be well stuffed off the back, particularly with high-withered horses.

The blinkers. The blinkers should be so fitted that the horse's eyes come almost in the middle of them, while the headstall should be tight enough to prevent the blinkers from bulging out when pressure is put on the bit, and thus enabling the horse to see behind him ; but they should be fitted so as not to turn inwards and almost touch the eyes. This is **Horse's** a point which is very often little attended **comfort** to, but one which makes a considerable **reflected in** difference to the horse's comfort, and is **manner of** **going.** naturally reflected in his manner of going.

The throat-lash should not be fastened too tight; if it is, it will half choke the horse. It **Throat-lash.** should be loose enough to allow three fingers to be passed between it and the horse's throat.

The nose-band should admit of the breadth **Nose-band.** of two fingers between it and the horse's jaw.

Bitting is all a matter of common sense and practice. The reins must be altered up or down the bit until the adjustment most comfortable for the horse has been discovered. But even then a great deal will depend on what is generally known as " Hands." This **Hands.** really unknown quantity, consisting as it does of complete sympathy between the horse and his driver, though born and not made, can be improved to some extent by teaching and practice. This gift has been defined as " not using more force on the reins than the exigencies of the occasion render absolutely necessary." As a general rule the bit should **Bitting.** lie flat in the horse's mouth about one inch above the tusks.

The curb-chain must not be too tight, **Curb-chain.** and there ought to be room for at least two fingers to be placed between it and the horse's jaw. If a horse is at all inclined to be a puller, an ignorant groom will very often fix it as tight as he can, with the probable result that the horse will jib or pull all the harder. In the latter case he will be likely to gct a sore under the jaw. The best remedy for this is to fix a piece of leather on the chain, so that the latter does not rub on the sore place. If a horse bores to the near side, putting the rein down lower on the off than on the near side will very often make him go straight, and *vice versâ*. Some horses pull with very sharp bits, and will not do so with a snaffle, while others do just the contrary. A double-ring snaffle covered with leather or made of india-rubber is useful for very light-mouthed horses.

Use of a net.   A net usually stops horses pulling for a time, but it is doubtful whether it has a permanent effect ; so that it is better to leave it off occasionally.

If a horse is inclined to put his head down, and bore, a bearing-rein will prevent him from doing so ; but it must not be too tight. There are many horses that would be un-drivable without one, as it keeps their heads in the proper position, and thus takes the weight off the driver's hand. When driving a young horse or a bad kicker it is always advisable to have a loose one on, as it will prevent him from becoming unmanageable by putting his head between his legs. The American pattern, which passes from the bearing-rein hook on the pad over the top of the horse's head, through a keeper on the headpiece between his ears, down to the bridoon is very useful for a hard puller.

Bearing-rein.

The correct adjustment of a bearing-rein requires a certain amount of practice, as when the horse is standing still it always appears much tighter than it really is.

Bitting of a pulling horse. Sometimes a very hard puller, especially in a team, can be driven with a big Liverpool bit hanging loose in his mouth and with the reins fixed to a bridoon ; a bearing-rein can also be fitted on this bridoon if required.

A martingale will prove effective in the case of horses who pull owing to their habit of star-gazing.

Sometimes a horse pulls by getting hold of the cheek of the bit with his lip. This can be met with the elbow-bit, which is an improvement on the Liverpool bit, as, by having a bend in it, the cheek is so far back that the horse cannot reach it with his lips or tongue. The reason that this bit is not more generally used is that many people consider it unsightly.

Indiarubber-covered bits, especially those

with a double bar, also answer very well with some pulling horses, the effect then being to make the bit work on a different part of the mouth from that to which they are accustomed.

A double bar can easily be improvised by sewing a piece of leather, like a lip-strap, only larger, across the top of an ordinary bit, just below the end of the headpiece.

An inveterate puller may in time get used to any bit, in which case frequent change is the only remedy.

In fact there is a key to almost every horse's mouth if it can only be found, and it is well worth taking considerable trouble to find it ; though frequently much patience and many experiments will be required before a successful result is obtained, and the man who has to drive many horses must have a large assortment of bits.

Every horse's mouth has a key.

Martingale.

A martingale is excellent for a horse that carries his head in the air, and also very effective for one that rears. It should be so adjusted as to keep the nose about in line with the withers, and is generally fixed to the nose-band, but may be attached to the bit, and when so attached it is better to use a half-moon snaffle, or one without a joint in it, as this greatly reduces the chances of the corners of the horse's mouth getting sore.

Cheek leathers.

Circular pieces of leather, called cheek leathers, are also very useful in this respect with ordinary bits, as they keep the corners

Corners of mouth sore.

of the horse's mouth from being pinched by the cheeks, and also prevent to a certain extent his getting hold of them with his lips.

One-sided mouth.

For a horse that has only one side to his mouth, it often answers to have a few tacks put on the inside of the piece of leather, which effectually stops him from leaning his head out to that side.

These pieces have a round hole in the middle, which fits the bar of the bit, and a slit from this hole to the outside, so that they can be put on and taken off quite easily.

Kicking-straps can be used either in single or double harness. In the former the strap passes up from one of the shafts through a loop in the crupper, and down to the other shaft. In double harness two straps are required. These are fixed to the pad, from which they run parallel to the crupper down to the splinter bar. They are connected by a short strap across the loins. Kicking-straps should be so adjusted that there should be plenty of room for the movement of the horse's quarters, as if he breaks into a canter they are liable to catch his quarters and so make him kick. A good rule is to allow

Kicking-strap

a hand's breadth between the horse's back and this strap.

Fitting of breeching.

A breeching is a necessity in a hilly country, more especially with a two-wheeled cart, when a brake is of no use. It should hang about a foot below the upper part of the dock, and have about four to six inches' play when the horse is in the collar.

Three kinds of breeching.

There are three kinds of breechings for a dog-cart.

The first starts from the tug on one end of the backband, and goes right round the horse's quarters to the tug on the other.

The second buckles to loops on each shaft, these loops being placed half way between the stops and the front of the cart.

Brown's patent.

The third consists of a broad strap, which is stretched fairly taut across the shafts about six or eight inches from the front of the cart. This one is always ready and requires no adjustment, looks neat, and answers admirably. It is known as Brown's patent.

The first method is better than the second, because it does not require any extra loops on the shafts, which tend to weaken them considerably, and also it does not take any of the paint off.

If a horse's quarters should get rubbed by the breeching, the best plan to prevent any further damage is to have a large piece of sheepskin sewn round the strap, with the hair next the horse. Breeching rubbing the horse.

The crupper ought to be fitted so that there is room for the breadth of the hand, or about four inches, between it and the horse's back, when the pad is in the right place. Great care should be taken that all the hairs of the tail are passed through the crupper. Crupper.

Breast harness can very often be sub- Breast harness.

stituted for collars with great advantage, especially when the horses' necks get wrung by the latter.

This method of draught also obviates the necessity of keeping a large number of collars to fit all sorts of horses, while another advantage is, that you are able to use breechings to the best advantage in double harness.

The breast strap should be made of a strong leather strap, about three inches wide, and padded inside so that the hard edges do not touch the skin.

For double harness a ring must be sewn into the middle for the purpose of attaching the pole chains.

The breast strap is held up by a light strap passing over the horse's withers, and the breeching, by a similar strap, passing over the croup. A crupper can be used, but is not necessary.

The breast straps should lie flat, and be kept well above the point of the shoulders. They must be carefully adjusted, the usual fault being that they are placed too low. Each end of the breast strap has a buckle, into which both the trace and the end of the breeching are fastened. Of course it is impossible to get as much work out of a horse with breast harness as with collars.

The whip should be as light as possible, Whip. and well balanced, the thong being about half the length of the stick. The points should always be of leather, as these are much the best in wet weather. A whip should never be allowed to stand in a corner or up against a wall, as it will very quickly warp in that position. It should always be kept hung up, either Always hang on a reel or by a string to a nail in the wall. whip up.

Before leaving the subject of harness, a word on the general appearance and neatness of turn-out will not be out of place. Straps ought to be shortened to fit the horse, and be no longer than absolutely necessary.

To prevent any ends flapping about, keepers must be tight, and fitted so as to be within an inch or two of the points of the straps. Nothing catches the eye more quickly, or looks more slovenly, than the ends of the traces sticking out a foot beyond the keepers, or a belly-band strap dangling loose underneath the horse.

When buying harness go to a really good maker : cheap clumsy harness never pays.

CHAPTER II.

DRIVING—SINGLE HARNESS.

BEFORE starting, always have a good look
round, and see that all the harness is put on
correctly ; then go to the off side of the horse
and take the reins in the right hand, the near
rein under the forefinger and the off rein
under the third finger. Get up into the
cart and sit down immediately ; now transfer the reins into the left hand, the near rein
over the forefinger, and the off rein under
the middle finger. Thus you have two fingers between the reins (fig. 2). The reason
for this is that it gives much more scope
for play of the wrist on the horse's mouth

than if you only have one finger between the reins. The thumb should point straight to the right, and the forefinger be held well

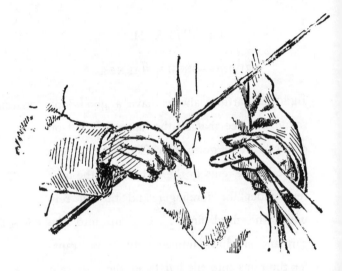

FIG. 2.—SINGLE HARNESS—POSITION OF THE HANDS.

out, pointing to the right rear. This will keep the near rein close up to the knuckle, and the horse may easily be moved across the road to either the left or right by turning the back of the hand up or down respectively.

Sit well up ; nothing looks so bad as to see the driver leaning forward over the reins. Sit well up.

Finally, take the whip in the right hand at the place where it balances most comfortably, and you are ready to start. Then give the horse the office to start by feeling his mouth gently and speaking to him ; if he does not respond touch him gently with the whip. How to start.

The moment he starts drop the hand slightly ; jibbing is often caused by neglect of the latter precaution.

Keep your elbows close to your sides, with the points almost touching the hips. The wrists should be well bent, as by this means you are enabled to keep a perfectly steady bearing on the horse's mouth without any jerking. This is a very important point. Elbows must be close to sides.

The fore arm should be horizontal, and the fingers from two to four inches from the centre of the body, with the knuckles to the front.

Fore arm horizontal.

The thumb must not be pressed down on the rein, exeept when a loop is taken up to turn a corner to the right or left (see fig. 23), when the right hand is available for shortening the other rein to prevent the horse turning too rapidly, or else to use the whip to bring him round.

Lower fingers to grip the reins.

How to turn.

The fingers which should grip the reins, (so tightly that they should never slip), are the three lower ones. The forefinger should be held as in fig. 2.

Never keep a large amount of slack of the off rein in your right hand (fig. 3), as then you cannot use the whip; and remember never to hit the horse while the right hand is holding a rein.

Whip not to be used when hand on reins.

The reason for this is obvious, because if you do try to hit him when you have the off rein in the right hand, you must slack

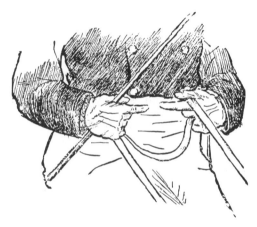

FIG. 3.—SINGLE HARNESS—RIGHT HAND IN WRONG POSITION.

that rein off, and the horse immediately dashes away to the left.

It cannot be too strongly impressed on the beginner, that whether the right hand is on the reins or not, they should always be of

Never move reins in left hand.

the same length in the hand, and never be allowed to slip.

The right hand should never on any account take the off rein out of the left hand. It is the first and most important law of driving, that the reins, as held in the left hand, should be of such a length as to keep the horse straight, and should remain at that length, whether the right hand is being used on one or other of them or not.

No coachman who drives with a rein in each hand can be said to know his business, and yet it is one of the commonest things to be seen in London.

Do not job horse's mouth.

Never use the whip on the horse unnecessarily, and never job him in the mouth except to punish him for doing something wrong. Nevertheless, for a horse which is inclined to kick, jobbing is very useful when applied at the right time, more especially if accompanied by a sharp hit with the whip over his ears.

The whip should never be used on a shier, it will only frighten him, and confirm him in the habit, which is caused by nervousness and not by vice. Encourage him rather by speaking to him, as there is nothing a horse learns to understand quicker than his master's voice.

Do not flap the reins on his back either to start him or to make him increase his pace.

Learn to drive at a steady and even pace. From eight to nine miles an hour will usually be found most suitable to average horses, but do not on any account drive sometimes at six miles and sometimes at ten. Nothing tires a horse so much as constantly changing the pace.

It is usually better to start a little slower, especially if you have a long way to go.

Never hit a shier.

Use the voice.

Pace should be steady.

Start slow.

Once fairly started, keep your eyes well fixed in front of you, and watch exactly what other vehicles are doing, so that you may never have to pull up suddenly. You should be able to see from a distance whether you can get through or not, and if you see that you cannot, begin to slow down at once.

Jerky pace very bad. Never increase your pace, or check it, suddenly. Nothing is more uncomfortable for the passengers or more wearying to the horse.

It is far better for the beginner to slow down at once, if he is not sure of getting through a tight place, than to go fast up to it, and then have to pull up quite suddenly, if he can pull up at all. This cannot always be done at the last moment, and an accident is **Shortening reins.** the result. As a rule, when it is necessary to pull up in a hurry, the reins cannot be shortened except by throwing up the hands, which, to say the least of it, looks very unbusinesslike. The proper course to pursue is to catch hold of the reins with the first finger and thumb of the right hand just behind the left, and shorten

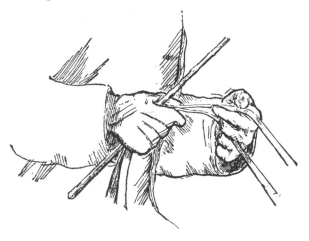

FIG. 4.—SHORTENING REINS.

them as much as necessary by pulling them through (fig. 4).

It is far better on such an occasion to have the reins rather too short than too long, but if only a small amount of shortening is required the right hand can be placed on the reins in front of the left and the left hand slid up to the right (fig. 5).

Signal with
whip to
carriage
behind.

When driving in a town, it is the rule to swing the whip stick round once or twice as an indication to the drivers of vehicles behind you that you are going to slow down or turn a corner.

Turn corners
carefully.

Before coming to the turn the pace must always be checked, particularly in a town, where the streets are generally slippery and there is nearly always a curbstone. Many an accident occurs daily through corners being negotiated carelessly. This advice appears almost superfluous, but the reader will find that to drive, even fairly broken horses, collectedly round sharp turns requires great care and precaution.

Starting a
jibber.

In conclusion, it is worth pointing out, that a horse which is inclined to jib, may often be started either by turning him to one side with the rein, or if this fails, by getting some one to push him over. The reason is that he is

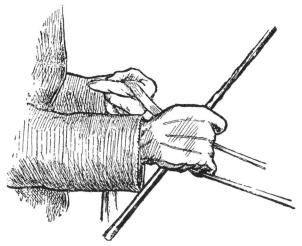

FIG. 5.—SHORTENING REINS BY SLIDING LEFT HAND UP TO RIGHT.

thus made to move before the pull comes on his shoulders.

The fit of the gloves may seem a very trivial matter to the uninitiated, but it is not considered such by the expert coachman.

Fit of gloves.

Any one attempting to drive with tight " masher " gloves will find his hand cramped in a very short time. All his power is taken up in trying to keep his hand shut and wrestling with his gloves, and not as it should be in holding the reins tight.

It is difficult in fact to have them too large.

They should be made of dogskin, and when new, at least one inch longer than the fingers, and rather larger, also very loose indeed across the palm of the hand and wrist. They will very soon shrink down and become the right size, after the hand has got damp in them once or twice.

It is a good plan to punch a few round holes in the back of the gloves to keep the hand cool.

The leather should be hard and tough, but not too thick. Strapping inside is apt to make gloves clumsy and very awkward for driving, especially with four reins.

Woollen gloves should always be carried, as they are the most comfortable in wet weather, and the reins do not slip through them. *Woollen gloves.*

Never drive without a rug or apron of some kind. A light cloth or cotton one may be used in summer, but for the winter it is far better to have a thick one of box cloth warmly lined. When choosing an apron, remember to get one with a V-shaped piece let in at the top ; this adds greatly to one's comfort if there are two people in the cart, as it allows of the sides being tucked under, and thus keeps out both cold and wet very much better than one without the V let into it. *Carriage rugs.*

A dog-cart is the handiest of two-wheeled carts for all-round purposes, and therefore the one in most general use ; so that a few hints on the selection or building of such a vehicle may *Hints on building dog-cart.*

be of use to those who have not had much practical experience in that line. At the same time I would strongly recommend that when buying a carriage of any kind professional advice should, if possible, be obtained, since no one without experience can possibly find out faulty workmanship or detect defects in the material.

The following would be built for horses about 15.2 in height :—

Height of wheels. The wheels should be fairly high, say about five feet, as this enables the horse to pull the cart over any small obstruction with greater ease than with low wheels.

Track of wheels. The track should be from five to five feet three inches wide. This gives plenty of room insi e, and makes the cart less likely to upset.

Bent shafts. Bent shafts are the most convenient for driving horses of different heights, and should be pivoted on the front part of the cart and

FIG. 6.—DOG-CART.

adjustable behind. A cart so constructed will easily admit of horses from 14.2 to 16 hands being driven in the same vehicle.

The body should be as wide as possible, because nothing is more uncomfortable than being cramped on a narrow seat. It also ought to be low on the axle, thus rendering the cart far more safe and also more comfortable. Body of cart should be wide and low.

A fixed body is better than one that moves backwards and forwards on the shafts, because it always remains the same distance from the horse, and enables the cart to be built lighter.

The seat should be low enough to prevent the driver from feeling he is in want of a foot-stool or that he is half standing, and should slide in a groove out of which it cannot come if the horse falls down. Many men have been thrown out and had bad accidents simply because of the seat coming away. It is more-over more comfortable if slightly below the Seat of cart.

top of the sides of the cart. The back and front seats should be so arranged that the cart will balance equally well with one person or four—a result which can be arrived at by having the seats to slide backwards and forwards when more than two people are in

the cart. I consider Heath's patent the best for this purpose ; it is very light and effective.

If the seat is a sliding one, the driver must

have an adjustable foot-rest, and this can easily be managed by having about half-a-dozen pairs of holes in the floor of the cart for the foot-rest to fit into.   It should be a plain board covered with indiarubber to prevent the feet slipping, and tilted at an incline which will keep the feet at right angles to the legs.

A bar foot-rest is most dangerous, as the fect may be easily caught under it in getting out

of the cart.   The lamps should be fixed

between the wheels and the sides of the cart, care being taken that there is plenty of room for them, so that should they get bent by any accident they will not interfere with the wheels. This position is much the best for tandem driving; in any other position they are continually catching the lash of the whip, and are consequently a perpetual source of annoyance.

The best system of draught for a dog-cart is that in which the traces are attached to a swingle-tree, from the centre of which two chains pass down to loops fixed to the axle close to the inside of the wheels. *Best trace attachment.*

The swingle-tree is held up by two straps which pass through metal loops in the front part of the cart. These straps should be pretty strong; were they to break, the bar would fall on the horse's hocks and cause an accident. *Swingle-tree*

Chains on
swingle-tree
not to be too
long.

Be careful that the chains are not too long, and that the pull is really on them, and not as is frequently the case entirely on the straps. In the latter case of course the swingle-tree ceases to be of any use.

Advantages of
swingle-tree
attachment.

The swingle-tree attachment enables the horse to pull directly from the axle-tree by means of the chains, and in this way the best line of draught is obtained ; moreover a certain amount of play is given to the horses' shoulders and the chance of their galling is less than with the ordinary method.

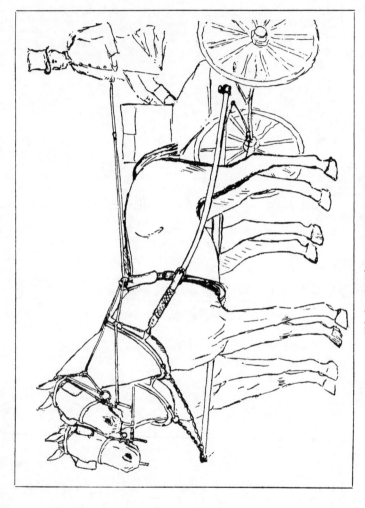

FIG. 7.—DOUBLE HARNESS ON HORSE.

CHAPTER III.

DRIVING—DOUBLE HARNESS.

To drive a pair well, that is, to be able to put-to and drive any two horses, is not such an easy thing as at first sight it may appear to the uninitiated. To drive a pair of good goers thoroughly accustomed to their work, and harnessed up in the right manner, is such a very simple matter that the merest tyro ought to be able to compete with it, with fair success. But when he has two entirely different and unknown animals to take in hand, it is quite another question.

Double harness is fitted exactly the same Belly-bands. way as single, except that the belly-bands should be slightly looser, so as to admit two or three fingers between them and the girths.

We will suppose that the harness has been put on the horses and correctly fitted to them, and that they are standing in the stable ready to be put-to ; then the correct way of bringing them out would be as follows :—

How to lead horse out of stable.

The traces having been placed across his back, the horse should be led out by the nose-band, not by the rein or the bar of the bit, otherwise the groom is very apt to job him in the mouth without intending to do so, a performance to which he may object and run violently back, or rear up and fall over. Great care should be exercised when leading out of the stable. It not infrequently happens that horses hit their hips against the walls, which is liable to chip them, and cause lameness, besides teaching them the extremely bad habit of rushing out of the stable-door.

Bring the horse carefully up alongside of the pole, so that he does not hit either the pole or the bar, and at once insert the hook of the pole chain into the ring of the kidney link of the hames, to prevent his running back on to the splinter bar.

Hooking in alongside of pole.

Now place the outside trace on the roller bolt, and afterwards fix the inside one. The quicker the latter is done with uncertain horses or kickers the better, as this operation renders it necessary to reach right over behind their quarters. If only one horse is likely to kick, he should be put in first, to avoid this danger. When taking out the exact reverse should always be adhered to.

Never pole up the horses too tightly, as it is very uncomfortable for them, more especially with a team, when the pole is a heavy

Polling up.

one, because if the pole chains are tight the weight of the pole will be always resting on their necks. See that the end of the hook on the chain is pointing downwards, as otherwise a horse with a bar across the bottom of his bit may get caught in it.

Pole pieces.

For ordinary pair work leather pole pieces are commonly used instead of chains. They do not require so much cleaning, and are much less trouble. They must be made of strong leather and kept soft with dubbing or salad oil, otherwise they may become rotten and dangerous.

Adjustment of coupling reins.

The correct adjustment of the two short inside reins, called coupling reins, requires great care. They should be so fitted that an even pressure is brought on both sides of the horses' mouths, and in such a way also that both horses shall go straight and pull evenly on the traces (fig. 8).

With a view to this the outer reins have a
number of holes punched in them, up and

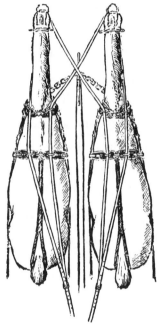

FIG. 8.—COUPLING REINS PROPERLY FITTED—HORSES'
HEADS STRAIGHT.

down which the buckles of the coupling reins
can be shifted, thus enabling them to be

shortened or lengthened to suit each particular horse's mouth.

For instance, if the near horse carries his head to the near side, the coupling rein on the off side should be taken up, when his head will be straightened. At the same time it must be borne in mind that if a coupling rein is let out the effect is also produced of shortening up the outer rein on the same side, and thus bringing the horse on that side further back than the other.

Supposing we have two horses apparently well matched, but that the near horse carries his head rather out to the front and has a light mouth, while the off horse has a hard mouth and carries his head close in to his chest. Now to get this pair to pull equally on the traces we must obviously have the near horse's reins considerably longer than those of the off horse. If they have been put to with the coupling reins of equal length, both buckled in the centre holes, there will then be three or four holes on each side of the buckles,

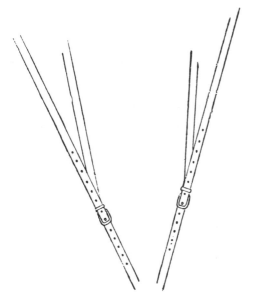

FIG. 9.—COUPLING REINS OF EQUAL LENGTH.

and the reins can either be let out or taken up (fig. 9).

In this case we should begin by letting out

the off side coupling rein two holes, and taking up the near side rein the same number (fig. 10).

Then as the near horse has a light mouth, he should be put on the cheek, and the hard mouthed pulling off horse on the middle bar. This fitting will probably suit the horses, and the pull on all four traces will be even.

The reins will now be adjusted like those in fig. 10, which shows how the near horse is able to hold his head well in front of the other, while the collars are brought level.

Coupling reins must not be too tight.   The most general fault is coupling up both reins too tightly, which makes the horses carry their heads in towards the pole, instead of going quite straight, as they should do. To prevent horses acquiring this habit, it is a good plan occasionally to change their positions, instead of always driving them on the same side of the pole.

This fault is very often to be seen in the leaders of a team, keeping them close to-

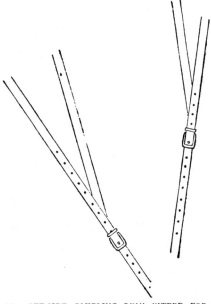

FIG. 10.—OFF-SIDE COUPLING REIN FITTED FOR HORSE
WHICH POKES HIS NOSE, NEAR COUPLING REIN FITTED
FOR HORSE WHICH CARRIES HEAD IN CHEST.

gether, and causing them to rub up against each other to such an extent that they some-times chafe.

It is a convenience, particularly when break-

To alter length
of rein without
interfering
with coupling
rein.

ing young horses, to have more than one hole in the billets for buckling the reins on the bits, so that a horse can be pulled back or let out a hole on either side without altering the coupling rein.

To prevent
horses leaning
against the
pole.

Horses in a pair sometimes get into the trick of leaning in against the pole, particularly when going down hill.

It is a difficult habit to cure them of, and perhaps the best preventive is a good cut with the whip when they first attempt it, though a little furze or a bit of hedgehog skin on the pole is sometimes effective.

Reins must not
be allowed to
slip.

Right rein
never be taken
out of left
hand.

The reins must never be allowed to slip through the fingers of the left hand, nor under any circumstances should the off rein be taken out of the left hand in order to turn to the right or pull across the road.

The right hand should pull the rein towards

the centre of the body, and not out to the side to which you wish to go.

Sometimes a horse gets galled by the collar, To prevent collar galling the wither. from being continually pulled up, or from holding back down steep hills; this can be remedied by having a tinned iron plate fitted on under the top of the collar, without taking the horse out of work.

It will be found that traces usually stretch Length of traces. and become of unequal length; when this occurs, the shorter trace should be put on the inside, and should be marked, so that it shall not be put on the outside by mistake. With some horses it will be found necessary to have the inside trace half a hole or even one hole shorter than the outer one, so as to obtain an equal pressure on both sides of the collar.

If bearing straps for the traces are used Bearing straps. they should be just long enough to keep them in a straight line; if longer, they will jump up when the horse goes into his collar.

Further instructions for his guidance in driving a pair the reader will find in the chapter on driving four horses.

Breaks are so commonly used in India, that a few hints may prove useful.

As a rule those in use are so low that the horses' quarters are in front of the footboard instead of being under it, and the driver is consequently too far from his work. In modern breaks the driving seat and boot are built almost exactly like those of a coach, where the footboard is well over the horses' quarters. That portion of the footboard which comes over the roller bolts should be about five feet from the ground, which gives room for the horses underneath.

The inside seats should be at least six feet long, so as to take four people comfortably on each side; a second seat behind the driving seat as on a coach can be added, and if necessary can be made removable. This gives three extra seats looking to the front, the occupants of which will not suffer so much from the dust as if they were inside.

The body can be hung on four elliptical springs, with a cross spring on the hind axle, or on two elliptical springs in front with two side springs and a cross spring behind. The latter method is to be preferred.

The approximate dimensions are as follows (see fig. 40): height of body from ground, 3 ft. 6 in.; driving seat without cushions, 7 ft.; front wheels, 3 ft. 2 in.; hind wheels, 4 ft. 6 in.; length of pole, 10 ft. 6 in.; weight about 12 cwt.; track, 5 ft.

Break measurements.

CHAPTER IV.

CURRICLE AND CAPE-CART.

WHEN it is desired to drive a pair, but owing to the expense, lack of carriage accommodation, or other reasons, the purchase of an extra carriage is inconvenient, an ordinary dog-cart can be fitted with a pole and adapted for a pair of ponies or horses at a very small cost. In such a case however the pole of the dog-cart, having nothing to support it with the ordinary double harness, would fall to the ground, and it would therefore be necessary to adopt one of the two following methods of draught :—

Curricle. 1. That known as Curricle, in which a bar passing from one horse to the other over the pads supports the pole by means of a strap or brace.

2. The system employed in what is generally known as the Cape-cart, in which the Cape-cart. supporting bar passes through a ring near the end of the pole, and is held up by straps passing over the horses' necks.

The first of these systems is the smarter in appearance, while the other is more suitable for rough work. I will begin by discussing the Curricle.

An ordinary dog-cart which has removable Cost of shafts can be fitted with the requisite gear, curricle. including the curricle bar and the pole chains, for about £10. The necessary alterations were made to my own dog-cart by Messrs. Heath of Aldershot, who had originally built it, but with no idea at the time it was made of having a pole eventually fitted to it. I found that it worked admirably from the first, and no subsequent alterations or repairs were necessary, there being in fact nothing at all likely to get out of order.

How to fit dog-cart with a pole.

To adapt the cart for pole draught, a large square iron loop must be fixed under the front of the cart, and a smaller one under the centre. The latter loop must be very strong and firmly fixed, as it has to take the extreme end of the pole, which at times puts on it a very great amount of strain.

An extra board will therefore probably have to be fitted right across the bottom of the cart, the ordinary boarding of which the bottom of a dog-cart is usually made being too thin and flimsy to resist the strain which the pole loop will put on it. Should this loop tear out, or the board to which it is fixed give way, a very serious accident may occur.

The pole must of course fit both loops

accurately, and it must be secured in them by a bolt passing through it and preventing it from being drawn out.

Underneath the pole at the point where the supporting strap will come there should be a strong spring (fig. 11), which will do away with much of the jar on the pole itself, and also on

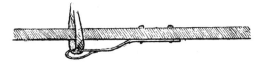

FIG. 11.—POLE FITTED WITH SPRING FOR CURRICLE.

the backs of the horses ; and if it is likely that a team of four will be driven, the pole should be made with a hook at the end to take the swingle bars.

For the attachment of the traces two bars must be provided for, and as the front of the cart will be too narrow for these to be fixed to it direct, iron stays projecting about six inches to either side can be screwed on underneath

Bars for attaching traces.

each end of the front of the cart. The bars can then be fixed to these stays by bolts passing through their centres. The bars will then revolve on their centres and give the horses' shoulders plenty of play, enabling them to do their work with much comfort.

To the dog-cart itself no other alterations are necessary. The addition of the pole does not affect the balance to any appreciable extent.

Difference between curricle and ordinary double harness.

With regard to the harness, the chief difference between curricle and ordinary double harness is in the pads.

These must be strong and heavy, and fitted with special roller bolts, on which the steel curricle bar rests (fig. 12). They require to be heavy and strong, because at times the pole will put a considerable weight on them, more particularly when going down hill.

On each side they have a leather loop like those on a tandem pad, and through these the traces are passed. In the bolts on the top of the pads is pivotted a small steel roller.

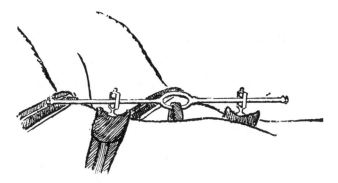

FIG. 12.—CURRICLE BAR AND ROLLER BOLTS.

The curricle bar rests on the rollers, and by their action is enabled to work freely from side to side, or from one horse towards the other, without any friction or noise. The rollers can be raised or lowered about a couple of inches, so that should the horses be of unequal height the bar can be levelled by raising or dropping one end of it.

Curricle bar.   The bar should be made of steel, and must be long enough to give at least six inches play to the outside of each pad when the horses are standing square in their places. It has a small screw at each end, on which are screwed flat circular nuts to prevent the bar dropping out of the bolts and off the rollers. These are put on immediately the bar has been passed through the bolts, and are themselves secured and prevented from coming unscrewed by V-shaped steel ties, which pass through slits at the extreme ends of the bar. In the centre of the bar is a long-shaped loop or slit, through which the brace or supporting strap is passed (fig. 12).

Supporting strap or brace.   This brace should be a strong leather strap about three inches wide. It passes under the spring below the pole, through the slit in the bar, and is fastened by a large double buckle.

The traces are the same as for single-harness.

To prevent the pole from tipping up when the weight is on the back of the cart, a light strap, with a double buckle at each end of it, can be fastened to the end of the girth-strap of one of the pads under the horse, passed over the pole, and again buckled at the other end to the other horse's girth-strap. This is an effectual remedy for the tilting up of the pole, even when a heavy man mounts suddenly on to the back seat. In all other respects the harness is the same as ordinary double harness.

If the cart is fitted with a swingle bar for single harness, the steel chains which connect the bar to the axle can perfectly well be used as pole chains, in which case

How to pre-vent pole tipping up.

it would be unnecessary to purchase new ones.

Ponies of fourteen hands or upwards, which would look too small for a full-sized dog-cart in single harness, and would be unable owing to its weight to draw it, look extremely well and make little of the weight when driven as a pair, and can thus be utilized in curricle when perhaps their services in harness would otherwise be lost.

A team of horses, or better still of ponies, can also be driven in the poled dog-cart, provided that the pole has the hook referred to before at the end of it.

Four horses look altogether too big, and the team is too long for the short cart behind it ; but a team of ponies, although they also look rather too long, are very much better ; and the slight disadvantage of appearance is well counterbalanced by the pleasure of driving them, and by the ease with which long distances can be covered without distress.

Given a good, comfortable, roomy dog-cart and four fairly-trained ponies which are really fit, and no more enjoyable way of travelling about a country can be found for two, three, or even four people. The weight to be drawn is so small compared to the horse-power employed, that all hills can be surmounted at a rapid pace, and long distances can be covered in a single day, without placing any undue strain on the cattle.

The bars, though considerably lighter, are exactly like the bars of a coach, while the leaders' harness, it is hardly necessary to remark, is precisely the same.

In the Cape-cart, about eighteen inches Cape-cart. from the end of the pole, comes a supporting bar or yoke, sometimes called a bugle, the use of which is to prevent the pole from falling to the ground. This bar, usually made of lance wood, about an inch in diameter, and five feet long, can be attached to the pole in several ways, but it is best so to arrange it that it can slide up and down the pole as well as from side to side. Perhaps the best and simplest attachment is obtained by passing a short strap with brass rings at each end of it round the pole, and then putting the yoke through the rings. The middle of the yoke ought to be covered with leather, to prevent it being chafed by the pole.

Though collars can be used, breast-harness is nearly always employed, and is much to be preferred on account of the breeching being much more effective than with collars ; without a breeching the horses are apt to come back on to the splinter bar.

Neither cruppers nor pads are essential.

FIG. 13.—CAPE-CART HARNESS.

The breast harness is held up by straps which pass through the same pads as the yoke straps.

These latter are fixed near the middle of the yoke, and pass through pads on the horses' withers to short buckling pieces attached near the outer ends of the bar.

Messrs. Atkinson and Philipson of New-castle-on-Tyne make a speciality of this kind of harness.

Makers of Cape harness.

A dog-cart can be adapted for the Cape-cart draught in exactly the same manner as previously described for curricle; the pole, however, should be rather longer.

Advocates of the Cape-cart claim the following advantages for it over the Curricle: that specially constructed heavy pads are not required, and that should one horse fall, there is very slight chance of his bringing down the other with him.

These two styles of draught are much used abroad, the latter in India, where it is known as "Tonga," the former in South Africa, whence it derives its name. As far as utility goes there appears to be little between them.

FIG. 14.—SPRINGING A HILL.

CHAPTER V.

DRIVING FOUR HORSES—POSITION OF COACHMAN.

IN order to learn to drive four horses as they should be driven, it is necessary to begin by studying the rules and general principles of this most fascinating amusement. To the lovers of this pastime nothing is more enjoyable than sitting behind a perfect and well-appointed team skilfully driven. It is most essential for one who would become a thoroughly efficient whip to have several years of constant practice, and even when this has been obtained, it will be found that there is still always something to learn.

Constant practice necessary.

For driving, like so many other accomplishments, requires to be kept up, or else the hand and eye will very soon be found to have lost their cunning, and not only does one become slow and clumsy with the whip and reins, but the arms and fingers soon tire.

Practice with weights.

In order to keep the hand in, when not driving regularly, an arrangement of weights and pulleys is a very convenient toy. It requires a weight of about twenty pounds (a cylinder of lead is very handy), to which is attached a strong cord. This passes over pulley P (fig. 15), fixed for convenience to the mantelpiece or other projection from the wall, down to pulley P¹, on the floor, and then ends in a loop, into which four straps can be fastened like reins. Then sitting in a comfortable chair, the hands holding the straps like reins, the weight can be kept working up and down (four or five inches will be found quite sufficient) for ten minutes or so. Another method, which is rather more complicated, but more useful for the beginner, is shown in fig. 16. This, while strengthen-

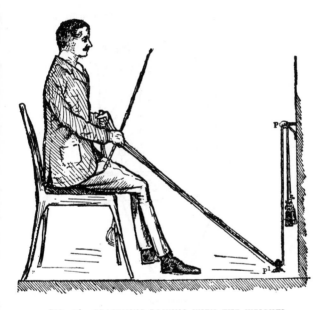

FIG. 15.—PRACTISING DRIVING WITH THE WEIGHTS.

ing his arms and fingers, enables him to acquire the art of looping and shortening the reins, and in fact to practise all the tricks of

Arrangement
of pulleys and
weights. the trade. For this practice eight pulleys
are required ; four are fixed on the wall, about
three or four feet from the ground and from
three to six inches apart ; the other four are

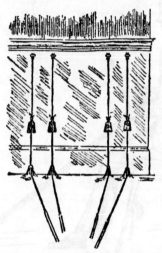

FIG. 16.—FOUR WEIGHTS AND PULLEYS FOR PRACTISING
DRIVING.

placed directly under these, and fixed to the
floor close up against the wall. A strong
cord is passed under each lower pulley first,
then over the pulley directly above, the ends

being fastened to weights of four or five pounds. To the other ends of the cords are attached leather straps similar to ordinary reins. Thus you have four reins, the two inner ones representing the wheelers, the two outer ones the leaders.

It has been found by trial that the approximate weight on the hands when driving a light team is about five pounds, but the average weight may be taken as about ten or twelve pounds, which will be much increased with a team of pullers ; while going down a steep hill the pressure will not infrequently exceed thirty-five pounds. These pressures, which I ascertained after many experiments, will show the novice how all-important it is that he should be really fit, and the muscles of his arms and fingers well developed, before he can hope to be really master of a team of horses.

Weight on hands when driving four horses.

It is always advisable, while practising with weights, to hold a whip, or stick to represent a whip, in the right hand, as by so doing you will very soon get into the way of using this hand correctly on the reins (fig. 15).

Muscle of thumb necessary for holding whip.

It is very important for the young driver to develop the muscle of the thumb ; otherwise it will be found extremely tiring to hold the whip properly for any considerable time, more especially against a high wind.

Messrs. Whippy and Steggall have shown me a very neat arrangement of weights and pulleys which can be easily fitted up in any room, and is well worth inspection.

Position of body on driving seat.

When driving, the body should be kept upright and square to the front, but all stiffness should be avoided. The driving seat should be low, and about three or four inches higher at the back than in front, so that the driver can sit down in a really comfortable position. The ankles and knees should be just

Position of legs.

touching each other, and the arms close to the
sides, the point of the elbows touching the
hip bone. The forearm should be about
horizontal, and the left hand from three to four
inches from the centre of the body, the back
of the hand being turned towards the front
and nearly vertical, but inclined a little towards
the horses. The wrist must be bent slightly
towards the body, and on no account allowed
to bend the other way. This is far the best
position for feeling the horses' mouths, as the
wrist then acts like a spring, and a perfectly
even pressure can be maintained. Sit well
back, and do not lean forward over the reins
in the attitude of a dairymaid on a milking-
stool. The driver should on no account be
half standing, or merely leaning against the
seat, with unbent knees, as, in the event of a
wheeler falling or shying up a bank, he will
inevitably be jerked off the coach.

Position of arms.

Position of left wrist.

Leaning forward bad.

Driver should sit well down.

CHAPTER VI.

FOUR HORSES—THE REINS.

How to hold
reins.

THE best way of holding the reins is to have
the near lead over the left forefinger, the off
lead between the forefinger and the middle
finger, the near wheel between the same and
under the off lead, and the off wheel between

Thumb and
forefinger
must not hold
the reins.

the middle and the third finger (fig. 17). The
reins must be gripped firmly by the three lower
fingers of the left hand, so that they cannot
possibly slip, the thumb and forefinger never
being used to hold the reins except when
looping. The thumb should invariably point
to the right, and the forefinger be held well
out. The near lead-rein should pass over or
close to the knuckle of the forefinger, and not

over the first or second joint. The beginner
will find that after a time the muscle at the

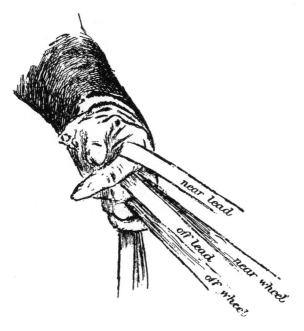

FIG. 17.—FOUR IN HAND—HOW TO HOLD REINS.

base of the left thumb will develop wonder-
fully, and that the reins will be held between

this muscle and the lower fingers very firmly without any apparent effort.

Adjusting
length of reins
in hand.

There are various ways of adjusting the reins, either by pulling them out or pushing them back from the front, or by pulling them from behind, or by taking out the lead reins.

Shortening
reins.

One general principle as to shortening the reins is to do it by putting the right hand in front of the left, and pushing those required to be shortened through the left hand. In doing this the thumb should never be used, as it is fully occupied in holding the whip. But the beginner will very often find it easier to shorten the reins from behind by pulling them through the left hand. In this case the thumb and forefinger must be used. I consider the following the easiest and most effective ways of adjusting the reins, viz. :—

To shorten all
four reins.

All four reins can be shortened, if much is required, by pulling them through from behind, but it is generally quicker and neater to hold the reins with right hand two or three inches in front of left (the little and the third fingers over the off-side reins and middle finger between the near-side reins), and then slide the left hand up to the right. By this means a perfectly steady pressure is kept on the horses' mouths. This movement is generally required when going down hill.

Both wheel reins.—It is better to shorten these by pulling them through from behind. This is necessary when going down steep hills, especially when the wheelers are loosely poled up, so as to prevent the bars hitting the leaders' hocks.

To shorten both wheel reins.

Both lead reins.—In order to shorten these take out both the leaders with the right hand (the third and little fingers over off, and first or middle finger over near-side rein); you can then pass them back to your left hand the

To shorten both lead reins.

required length by letting them slide through the right hand the necessary amount. To lengthen them, simply pull them through from the front.

Shortening
near-lead
rein.

The near lead.—Either push through from the front, with the full of the right hand over the rein, or take it right out of the left hand the same way and replace it the proper length.

Shortening off
lead rein.
Shortening
near wheel.

The off lead.—Push through from the front.

The near wheel.—This rein will be found the most difficult of all to keep in its right place and to shorten. It constantly slips when the horses pull, and for beginners it is certainly the best plan to pull it through from behind. It can also be done by lengthening out the off-lead rein from the front, and then pushing both reins back together.

Shortening off
wheel.

The off wheel.—Push it through from the front with the right hand.

The two centre reins.—Always adjust them from the front. If the leaders are not straight in front of you, which will be found a very common occurrence, but are running to the right, they will generally come straight by pulling the two centre reins through the left hand from the front, so as to lengthen them a little ; on the contrary, if the leaders are running to the left, push these two reins back so as to shorten them.

If, however, they are going to the right or left simply because you are holding the off or the near-lead rein too short, let out this rein only, just enough to bring the leaders square.

The following are probably the easiest and most effective methods of passing off across the road, or of turning to the right or left :—

1. *To the left.*—Turn the left-hand knuckles

upwards, and pass it across the body from left to right; the horses will incline to the left, the reins on that side being shortened.

To the right.—Pass the left hand down towards the left hip, back of the hand to the front, with the knuckle of the forefinger downwards and that of the little finger uppermost; this shortens the right-hand reins and causes the team to incline in that direction. The whip can be applied to the off-wheeler in the first instance, or the near one in the second, in front of the pad, if the horses do not cross rapidly enough.

2. *To the left.*—With the right hand seize the near-lead and wheel reins under the lower fingers; then either pull those reins up towards the centre of the body, which will shorten them, or allow the left hand to go slightly to the front, which will slack off the right reins, or better still, combine both these motions,

the result being the same in each case, that
the team will go to the left.

To the right.—Take hold of the off-lead
and wheel reins with the lower fingers of the
right hand, and treat them in the same way as

FIG. 18.—STEADYING TEAM WITH RIGHT HAND.

described for the left reins, when the team will
go to the right.

The latter of the two methods is by far the
best and the one most usually employed, the
other only being possible with very perfectly

broken teams, as obviously only very little pressure can be put on.

To steady the team.   In order to steady the horses or to ease the

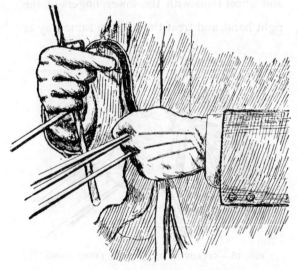

FIG. 19.—HOW LOOP SHOULD BE TAKEN UP.

left hand, the right hand may be placed in front of the other over all the four reins (fig. 18), but it is generally preferable to have the hand on only three reins for steadying purposes, the

third and little fingers being over the off reins
and the upper fingers over only one of the
near reins.

It will now be necessary to explain the The point or
loop.
term " point " or " loop." The point is made

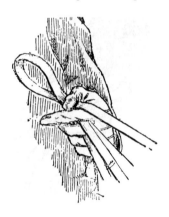

FIG. 20.—LOOPING NEAR-LEAD REIN UNDER THUMB.

by taking hold of either the near or the off-
lead reins under the little and third fingers of
the right hand (not with the forefinger and
thumb), and placing it six inches or more
(according to the inclination of the turn),

in advance of the left, and then bringing it
back so as to form a loop under the left thumb
(figs. 20, 21), which must press the rein firmly
down on the forefinger. As a rule never move
the left hand forward while doing this. The

FIG. 21.—LOOPING OFF-LEAD REIN UNDER THUMB.

off-lead rein can also be looped under the first
finger in turning to the right (fig. 22).

Turning to either side can be done as
follows : By pointing the near leader to turn
to the left (fig. 20), or the off leader to turn

to the right (fig. 21); or, by pointing both the
near-lead and the near-wheel reins together to
go to the left, and similarly both the off-side
reins together to go to the right, at the same

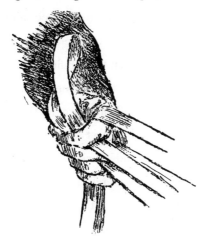

FIG. 22.—LOOPING OFF-LEAD REIN UNDER FIRST
FINGER.

time striking the opposite wheeler with the
whip in front of the pad after the point has
been made, if the horses are required to move
in either direction very quickly; or, by passing

the near-wheel rein round the left thumb, and then looping the off-lead under the fore finger (fig. 22), it will be found that the horses will get more easily round a very sharp and

Turning an
awkward
corner.

awkward corner to the right, especially going down hill. In a like manner, by looping the off-wheel rein under the forefinger of the left hand, and then pointing the near leader under the thumb, any difficult turn to the left can be negotiated with perfect safety. This method will often be found quicker and better than passing the off-wheel rein under the thumb.

Meaning of
opposition
point.

This looping up of the wheeler's rein on the opposite side to which you are about to turn may be termed the " Opposition point."

This device for preventing the wheelers from cutting the corners will be found most useful with horses that have been driven a great deal in the wheel, because they soon learn to recognize the indication given to the leaders by the shortening of the lead rein passing along close to their heads.

Very often, when the wheelers are boring to one side going down hill, and the whip is

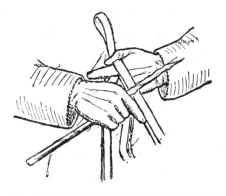

FIG. 23.—RIGHT HAND ON OFF-SIDE REINS TO PREVENT
WHEELERS CUTTING CORNER.

required, it is useful to loop up the wheeler's rein on the opposite side to which they are boring, before using the whip.

Be careful, when stretching out the right hand in order to take up the lead rein to loop Do not lean forward when looping.

it, not to lean the body forward, as it looks very bad, and almost invariably shows that the left hand is holding the reins too short and is too far away from the body.

It is a common fault with beginners to stretch out the left hand when looping, thus taking up a larger loop than would be necessary, if the left hand had a proper hold of the horses' heads.

The loop once made should not be allowed to slip until the turn is completed.

The right hand, having once caught up the loop, and given the leaders the office which way to turn, is then free to be used in any of the following ways : to seize both the off-side reins, if turning to the left, to prevent the wheelers from going too quickly round the corner (fig. 23) ; to assist them, if not turning sharply enough, by catching hold of the near-side reins ; to do just the opposite if turning

Prevent
wheelers
cutting
corners.

to the right; or finally to use the whip on either of the wheelers, by hitting the outside one to make them come round more quickly, or the

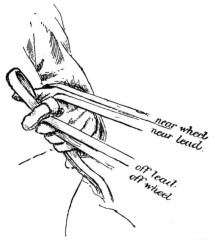

near wheel
near lead.

off lead.
off wheel

FIG. 24.—OPPOSITION POINT TO THE RIGHT.

inside one to prevent them cutting the corner.

More than one point can be made, if a large enough loop has not been taken up at first, but usually one point is sufficient, enough rein being taken up the first time to complete the turn.

Looping a second time, when first loop not enough.

Sometimes at a very sharp corner two points are necessary, as you may find that the first one is not bringing the leaders round fast enough.

Opposition point to right.

The opposition point to the right is made by putting the near-wheel rein round the left thumb, passing it from inside from right to left, and then making the point with the off-lead rein under the forefinger (fig. 24). When once round, first let go the point of the leader, and then that of the near wheeler. Conversely,

Opposition point to left.

the opposition point to the left is made by putting the off-wheel rein under the forefinger of the left hand, and then pointing the near-lead rein under the thumb (fig. 25). In order to avoid having two reins looped up under the thumb, it seems better to use the forefinger for one of the loops and the thumb for the other ; in this manner either loop can be let go separately.

It should hardly ever be necessary to shorten the lead reins when going down hill, as the mere fact of the wheelers coming back

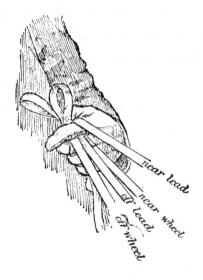

FIG. 25.—OPPOSITION POINT TO THE LEFT.

out of draught to hold back the coach will make you shorten up the reins enough to bring the leaders out of draught at the same time. If anything, it will be found necessary to shorten the wheel reins, more especially if the hill is very steep and the wheelers are loosely poled up.

Leaders out of draught going down hill.

Going down hill the leaders should just carry the bars, and nothing more. They should not put any strain at all on the pole, for by doing so they obviously tend to counteract the efforts of the wheelers to keep back the coach. In order to carry the bars the traces should be slack, but not slack enough to let the whole weight of the bars weigh down on the pole, which would put so much extra weight on the wheelers' necks.

Leaders must not pull on pole when turning.

Be careful that the leaders are not straining on the pole when turning a corner, as otherwise the wheelers will inevitably be pulled sharply across on to the pavement or footpath, and the pole may be broken.

CHAPTER VII.

FOUR-IN-HAND—THE WHIP.

YOU must learn to play with the whip neatly, How to hold whip. and to be able to use it skilfully on any of the horses. The handle should rest in the palm of the right hand, and be kept firmly in its place by the action of the thumb pressing against the base of the forefinger ; the lower fingers will then be left free to catch hold of the reins.

If, however, it is necessary to pull the reins through from behind, the lower fingers must be tightened on the handle so as to allow the thumb and forefinger to be used.

Always take care that the whip is in its right place, and the thong properly done up.

Angle of whip. Hold the whip at an angle of about thirty degrees to the left front and about forty degrees upwards, and not as in the picture opposite (fig. 26).

The thong ought to have three or four turns round the stick, the first turn beginning close to or on the quill, which is always covered with black twine.

No kinks in lash. Pay special attention to holding the whip so that the double thong hangs straight down and has no kinks in it. If there should be any kinks they can be taken out by adding a turn or two on the stick, or by taking some off.

Do not hold the whip tighter than is absolutely necessary. In fact, when the hand is on the reins the grip may be released altogether for a time, as they will hold it up ; this will give the thumb a rest. Holding it loosely also ensures the double thong hanging straight down, as then it will do so by reason of its own weight. It looks excessively bad to see the whip held all sideways, but it will con-

FIG. 26.—RESULT OF HOLDING WHIP IN WRONG POSITION.

stantly get into that position unless the tyro pays great attention to keeping it straight.

The point of the lash should be just under the inside of the thumb ; this will keep it from Lash of whip under thumb.

slipping. Hold the whip where it balances comfortably, the end of the stick close to, and under the forearm, the wrist well bent, and the elbow close to the side.

Position of whip hand.

When the right hand is not on the reins or using the whip, it should be kept close to the left, the forearm being about horizontal. It can then rest on the thigh, and yet be ready for any emergency.

Balance of whip.

A good whip should balance well when held at or close to the collar (this should come nearly under the thumb), otherwise it will be found top-heavy and clumsy.

The collar is the plate about ten inches from the thick end of the stick, and is sometimes termed the top ferrule.

Choice of whip.

In choosing a whip the most essential points are : firstly, that it should balance as above ; secondly, that it should be fairly light and springy—springiness being useful, because it

renders a whip very much easier to catch ; and,
thirdly, that it should have some knots near

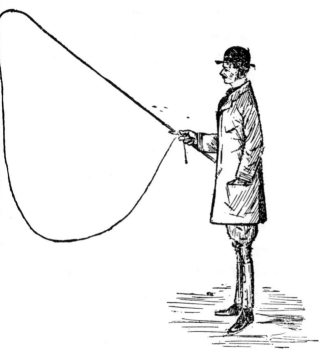

FIG. 27.—PREPARING TO CATCH THONG.

the top, as they materially assist in keeping
the thong up, though too many will be

found an impediment to getting it out quickly.

How to catch thong of whip.

A very good way to learn to catch the thong neatly round the stick is this : chalk a large pot-hook or *S* on the wall ; stand opposite to this with the whip held in the proper position, the thong undone, and the point of the lash under the middle finger of the right hand, the forefinger rather pointed up the stick (fig. 27) ; then with the point of the whip quickly follow the line as traced on the wall, beginning from the bottom end, and moving it across from left to right ; the top part of the *S* should be done by a back turn of the wrist, first upwards and then downwards, which will bring the fingers uppermost at the finish.   Never let the point of the whip drop at the beginning of the *S*, and never hit at the thong, but on the contrary make it come up to the stick.   If you find that the thong is caught rather too low down, it can be very easily sent up higher by catching it again as above, but with rather a shorter

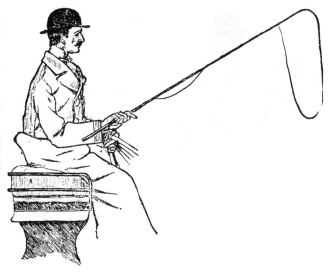

FIG. 28.—THONG CAUGHT UP BEFORE LOOP HAS BEEN TAKEN OFF.

and more jerky motion, in fact describing a small *S*.

This is done almost entirely by the wrist, with only a slight movement of the arm.

Taking out
loop in lash.

Having caught the thong (fig. 28), the next thing to be done is to take out the loop which will be found in the middle of the stick, so

FIG. 29.—TAKING OFF LOOP.

that all the turns should be from right to left; otherwise it will very soon come undone. To do this, lower the stick so as to enable the left thumb to seize the loop (taking care not to move the left hand from its correct position while doing so) ; now move the whip hand out to the right front as far as possible, keeping the wrist well bent and holding the lash tight with the left thumb (fig. 29). This movement will take off the turns on the lower end of the stick. Now place the whip under the left thumb, and turn the spare end of the lash once or twice round the handle (fig. 30). With the right hand retain the point of the lash securely under the inside of the right thumb, which will prevent the thong getting loose. If the point slips up, it can be pulled tight again by catching hold of it with the left thumb and forefinger, and drawing the right hand away.

End of lash round handle of whip.

The thong should be kept pliable by being rubbed with salad oil or mutton fat ; otherwise it will be found difficult to keep it in its proper place when caught.

How to keep lash pliant.

The following rules should be followed in hitting the horses :—

How to hit horses with whip.

The wheelers should be hit in front of

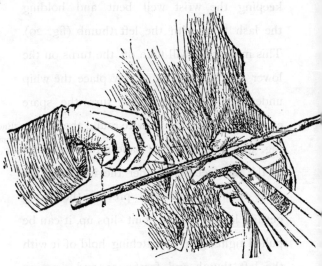

FIG. 30.—SECURING LASH BY TWISTING IT ROUND
HANDLE OF WHIP.

the pad to avoid making them kick. If ever they should attempt to kick, a severe blow about the ears will usually put a stop to it. Generally move the whip from left to right, keeping the wrist nearly stiff, and doing it as far as possible from the elbow, without any circular motion of the forearm. With a fidgety near wheeler it is advisable to hit the off one on the outside. It is no use hitting the wheelers if the leaders' reins are too long ; in this case you must first shorten up the leaders' reins, and then use the whip on the wheelers ; otherwise, as soon as the wheelers have jumped into their collars, the leaders will again press forward, and allow the wheelers to hang back as before.

The best way to hit the off leader is first to bring the top of the whip from the near to the off side of the coach ; then undo the thong by swinging the stick round and round, at the same time keeping the point of the lash under the first finger. Next bring the right hand down close to the left, and place the left thumb over the point of the lash so as to

Hitting off leader.

keep it clear of everything. Now swing the stick back to the right until the wrist is about in line with the shoulder, at the same time releasing the point from under the thumb. This should be done with very little movement of the wrist. Make a good circular turn and bring the stick to the front again sharply, aiming with the point a little in front of the spot you wish to hit. In doing this the lash can travel to the front either above or below the stick, but in traffic, or when under trees, the latter will be found the safer.

The only place the point of the whip should ever crack is on the horse, and never under any circumstances in the air, which would be dangerous, especially to those on the back seat, besides being very unworkman-like.

The lash should hit the leaders under the bars on their hocks, as it does not look well to see wheals or streaks of mud on the horses' flanks and quarters.

To hit the near leader, begin as before, but instead of making the lash go to the off side of the coach, throw the right hand well up and make a good swing with the stick, so that the lash may go well over the heads of the passengers from the off to the near side, and then by dropping the point of the stick and letting the hand go slightly out to the front, it will be found that the lash will swing in and hit the near leader, while passing outside and avoiding the near wheeler's head. Hitting near leader.

Having once hit the leader, the lash should be brought back on the near side of the coach. Do not attempt to get it straight back to your hand, otherwise you will most likely hit the wheeler, or the passenger on the box seat, but just send the lash out to the front over the leaders with a circular motion, and then by Bringing back lash.

holding the stick nearly upright it will come into your hand or under your arm (fig. 31). This will leave the right hand free to steady the horses, which will generally be found necessary. The lash, having been brought back to the near side of the coach, can also be recovered by raising the whip vertically and bringing it over the wheeler's back.   This, although a quicker plan than the other, will not be found so easy or so safe.

Hitting near leader under bars.

The near leader can also be hit from the off side under the bars.   To do this the lash must be thrown outwards, away from the coach, and then brought back swinging under the stick, so that the point passes between the off wheeler and the off leader just under the end of the pole.   This requires a considerable amount of practice, otherwise the off-side horses will often be hit by mistake. Another very useful method is to throw the

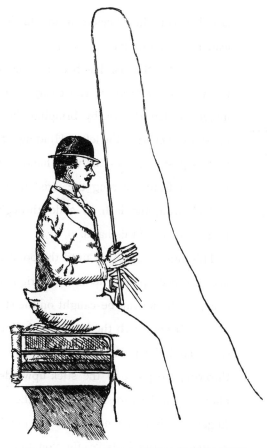

FIG. 31.—BRINGING BACK THONG OF WHIP AFTER
HITTING A LEADER.

lash between the wheelers' heads, hitting the leader on the quarter.

When once the lash has been secured under the wrist or forearm, it can easily be placed under the left thumb by bringing the right hand down close to the left. Holding it firmly in this position, draw the whip hand away to the right front, keeping the wrist well bent, and allowing the lash to slide through the middle finger of this hand.

Placing lash under thumb before catching up.

This can be repeated until the point of the lash has been pulled up into the right hand, when the thong can be caught on the stick as usual. If you catch the lash straight into the right hand the point may be got hold of by throwing the point of the stick upwards, and allowing the lash to slide through the middle finger. This is not nearly such a good plan as that described above, for you may easily throw the lash away altogether, and thus have to catch it again. Be careful, when you have the point of the lash in the right hand, to see that the loop is well clear of everything before catching it up on the stick, as it often gets caught round the handle of the footboard or against the reins, which utterly spoils the catch. You should never hit a horse with the whip while the right hand is holding a rein ; it looks very awkward, and is most unworkmanlike. Should you have a loop of a rein in the right hand, as you might have when going round a corner to the right, first place the loop under the left thumb or forefinger, and then use the whip.

See that thong is not caught on footboard.

Never use whip when right hand on reins.

If when hitting a leader the lash should get caught round the bars or harness, do not jerk or pull it hard, but shake it loosely up and down ; otherwise it will most likely get caught all the tighter.

To release lash caught in harness.

If you want to use the right hand on the

Whip under thigh.

reins while the lash is caught, place the handle under the thigh and sit on it. Should

Lash caught in tree.

the whip get fast in the bough of a tree or a lamp-post, on the near side, the only thing to do is to let it go at once, letting your hand go well up and over to the left. You will then avoid hitting the passenger on the box seat. Constant practice with the whip is absolutely essential ; no one can drive well until he has thorough control over it, and is able to manipulate it in such a way that the horse struck is the only one which knows that it is being used.

CHAPTER VIII.

FOUR-IN-HAND. STARTING—PULLING UP— TURNING.

BEFORE starting have a good look round and see that the horses are properly put in, that the harness is correctly put on and fitted, and more especially that the bits are rightly adjusted and the reins put in the correct places. Take care also that the pole-pin is in its place. It is never safe to trust entirely to the servants or ostlers.

Looking round before starting.

The lead reins should never under any circumstances be buckled together ; the reason of this is that if the main bar gets broken, the leaders will be able to pull the reins through and get clear away. On road coaches it is

Lead reins should never be buckled.

customary to leave both lead and wheel reins unbuckled.

Place the whip neatly caught up in the socket, if not already there. Standing alongside of the off wheeler's quarters, with the right hand take hold of the leaders' reins without touching the horses' mouths, and place them in the left hand, the forefinger between them ; next take hold of the wheelers' reins, placing the middle finger of the left hand between them, without pulling them so tight as to feel their mouths.

Preparing to start—taking up reins.

Then with the right hand pull out the off-side reins twelve to eighteen inches, and see that the splicing on the lead reins and the buckles of the couplings in the wheel reins are about the same distance from the left hand. The reins will then be about level when you are seated on the box.

Having done this, transfer the four reins to the right hand, but one finger lower down than they are held in the left; the first finger will then be free to hold on to the footboard whilst climbing up.

Transferring reins to right hand before mounting box

In order to help yourself on to the box, catch hold of the lamp wire with the left hand, place the left foot on the pipe box of the wheel, the right foot on the roller of the splinter bar; then the left foot can be raised on to the step and the right foot on to the footboard.

Mounting box seat.

Now sit down on the seat at once; otherwise if the horses start off suddenly you may be pitched off. Immediately transfer the reins from the right hand back to the left, by passing the fingers of the left hand just in front of the fingers of the right, the forefinger of the left hand being opposite the middle finger of the right. Then adjust any rein not found to be

Sit down at once when mounted.

Rug or apron necessary.

correct. It is always advisable to have a rug or apron over your knees, as not only does it look untidy to be without one, but it also saves your trousers immensely, as the reins are sure to touch them to a certain extent and wear them out, especially in damp weather. As soon as you have arranged the reins satisfactorily in the left hand, being especially careful not to have them too long, take the whip out of the socket and keep it in the right hand. Before starting always give the caution, "Sit fast," or ask if "All right behind?" as many a man has been jerked off from not knowing that the coach was going to start.

Caution to passengers before starting horses.

To start horses.

To start, feel all the horses' mouths, and, if necessary, give them the word to go, dropping the hand to them at once until the coach is fairly off. Nothing tends more to make horses jib than holding on to their heads at the moment of starting. The wheelers ought Wheelers start the coach. to start the coach, and this can be effected by touching them with the whip if they require a hint. Do not, however, on any account hit a wheeler which is inclined to jib, but make the others get the coach moving.

To be able to start horses well is perhaps the most difficult thing which the young driver has to learn. The knack can only be acquired by experience, and no absolute rules can be laid down for his guidance, as no two teams are alike in temper and disposition.

Before starting have the rugs taken off quietly, not snatched off, and, as soon as you are ready, make the grooms stand well clear of the horses' heads. Then start them as quietly as possible, devoting all your skill to getting the coach under weigh at once, without pulling at the horses' heads, as nothing rritates horses so much, or is more apt to make them jib, than jerking their mouths, or having to pull up and start afresh. As soon as they are well started, you can bring your hand back a little and feel their mouths properly. Then if you find that the horses are not going straight you must re-adjust the reins as quickly as possible ; this is a most difficult thing for a beginner to do neatly. It is a good plan to start with the near-wheel rein rather shorter than the off, as that is the most difficult rein to shorten in a hurry.

Whip should be in the hand, ready for use at start.

It is never safe to start the coach without having the whip in the right hand ready for immediate use. The whip is to the driver what the leg is to the rider, *i.e.*, it keeps the horses up to their bits.

As soon as the horses are going straight take the right hand off the reins, at the same time keeping it close by ready for any emergency.

A great deal of the neatness in driving depends on what may be termed the give and take of the left hand. That is, it can be allowed to go forward or be lowered a little, or be pulled back close to the body ; for instance, in order to pull across the road to the right, the right hand should pull the off side reins, while the left hand at the same time moves slightly to the front so as to slack off the near side reins. In this way both hands do their share of the work, and an exaggerated movement of the right hand is rendered unnecessary. Much can also be done by turning the back of the left hand either up or down. The principal effect of this is to shorten or lengthen the near-lead rein, and so pull the leaders more or less across the road.

Left hand must give and take.

When you want to pull up, shorten all the four reins by passing the left hand up to the

Pulling up.

right, or else by pulling all the four reins through from behind as before explained ; then having the right forefinger on the near-lead rein, the middle finger on the near wheel, and the lower fingers of the right hand on the off reins (see fig. 35), pull both hands back towards the body, and if necessary lean back a little. It is not easy to pull up exactly square, as one wheeler will very often hang back much more than the other. This can be regulated by pulling rather harder with the middle finger to keep the wheelers to the left, or by pressing strongly with the lower part of the hand, in order to keep them to the right.

Should the horses be getting the better of you, and you find that you cannot stop them, it will be found a great assistance to place the right leg over all the four reins, as you may then be able to stop them by the extra power and leverage you gain by the position of the leg.

Having pulled up at the end of a stage, professional coachmen always throw the reins down with both hands outside the wheelers.

With plenty of room a coach can be turned round at a considerable pace, but for this a wide sweep must be taken.

When turning round, go slow.

Unless there is at least twenty yards, re member to go very slowly; otherwise the coach may lock, and then nothing can save it from overturning except the breaking of the pole.

Coach may lock and upset.

In any case great care must be taken to keep the wheelers well out and the leaders' bars very slack. To do this it is well to put on the opposition point, and take a large loop in the leaders' reins.

If it is necessary to turn in a very narrow road, it is generally better to take the leaders

Turning in narrow road.

out, but it can also be done in the following manner :—

Pull off to the left side of the road as far as possible, and then pull up to a walk; slant the horses across the road to the right by advancing a little, and then halt, pulling strongly on the near reins so as to get the pole across to the left; shorten up all the reins, and with the little finger of the right hand on the off-side reins, and the middle finger on the near-wheel rein, pull back the horses, backing the coach as far as circumstances will admit. When again halted the coach ought to be at right angles to the road. The leaders must now be brought right round to the right, and in order to do this it is usual to shake the off-lead rein a little before taking up the loop, otherwise the leaders may come back on to the pole.

The wheelers must be brought round after

Backing coach to enable turn to be made.

the leaders, care being taken not to bring them round too quickly, so as to lock the fore-carriage. Turning to the left is done in a similar manner. With unsteady horses it is safer to take out the leaders, as they are apt to be hit by the bars, or come back on the pole.

Always pull the reins that you take up with the right hand towards the centre of the body, and on no account let your hands move across to the side to which you want the horses to go. This rather appears to be the natural tendency, but it must be overcome. It is often unnecessary to loop when going round a gentle curve, and it may be sufficient to pull the lead rein with the right hand, and then, while still retaining a slight bight in it, to catch hold of the wheel rein on the same side just below ; by this means you pull both the reins on the same side, but with greater

Pull of right hand should be towards centre of body.

Turning corner without looping.

force on the lead rein than on the wheel.
This plan may also be adopted for slanting
across the road.

CHAPTER IX.

FOUR-IN-HAND. VARIOUS USEFUL HINTS—
WHAT SPARE ARTICLES TO CARRY, ETC.

THE beginner must not suppose that a team, or for that matter even one horse, can be driven with the left hand only ; even the very best of whips is obliged to have constant recourse to the right hand, especially when passing through traffic.

At the same time, he must remember to resist the temptation of keeping the right hand permanently on the reins, nor should it ever be employed like the coachman's hand in fig. 3, in holding on to a bight of the off reins in order to keep the horses straight.

The team ought to run perfectly straight at any time with the reins in the left hand only ; and as a continuous pressure of the right hand is very liable to cause any one of the reins to slip, especially the near wheel when the horses are pulling, this practice is objectionable. Of course if the left hand gets tired, the right must come to its assistance, and then it should be placed either on three or all four reins (see figs. 18 and 35).

Always keep a steady pressure on reins.

Mind and keep a good steady pressure on the reins at all times, and keep the horses up to that pressure with the whip. The most common fault among amateurs is that they do not hold their horses nearly tight enough by the head. Always have a good hold of

Reins slipping a common fault.

them, and above all things remember never to let the reins slip through the fingers. This is a constant cause of horses getting out of hand, and pulling for a long way, when they would otherwise have gone quite comfortably after the first mile or so.

To prevent the reins from slipping, if the horses are pulling, and especially with new gloves, it will be found very convenient to put a little powdered resin or beeswax on the fingers and palm of the hand. *Resin or wax on gloves.*

If you have time, always start slowly (at first six or seven miles an hour); by adopting this plan the horses will go more kindly, and after a bit your arm and fingers will feel much less tired than if you had started at a rapid pace. *Start slow.*

It is very important to keep the right wrist well rounded when pulling the reins on either side, and the back of the hand rather inclined downwards. *Right wrist well rounded when right hand on reins, back inclined downwards.*

By keeping the hand in this position it will be found that the point of the whip is kept well to the front and high up. If the back of *Point of whip to be kept well up and to the front.*

the hand is turned up at all, the whip is sure either to cause considerable inconvenience to the person on the box seat (fig. 26), or else to hit the near wheeler close to his tail. This will most probably make him swish it, and if it should by any chance get over the thong, the result may be disastrous to the boot.

Team boring to one side— how to remedy.

If the horses are all boring to the left, it is no use simply pulling at the two off-side reins with the right hand, but at once shorten these reins in the left.

This can be done either by shortening them singly, or by catching hold of the two off-side reins as usual, placing the forefinger over the near lead, and the middle finger over the near wheel, and then allowing the near-side reins to slide a little through the fingers of both hands, while still retaining a firm grip of the off-side reins. Of course, however, only a very little can be got out at a time by this method.

Another plan is to grip the reins tightly with the right hand, the first two fingers over the near-side reins, the lower fingers over the off, and then to open the fingers of the left hand, when the off-side reins can be pushed through them by turning the lower part of the right hand towards the left (see figs. 18 and 35).

Never on any account take the left hand out of the reins, even though the right may be holding them firmly in front, as it is very difficult to get the left hand back into its place again with the reins in the right places. Of course, if your fingers are numbed from cold or from hard pulling, it will be necessary to take the hand out and slap the fingers on the thigh. But if the horses seem to be going all anyhow, take the leaders out with

Never remove left hand from reins.

Taking leaders' reins out with right hand.

the right hand, the little finger over the off lead, and the first or second finger over the near lead (fig. 32) ; then adjust the wheelers by letting the rein which is too short slide gently

Lead reins
should seldom
be removed
from left
hand.

through the left hand, and replace the leaders If the reins are found to be too long, shorten them all from behind. This plan should be rarely resorted to, as it is a very bad habit to perpetually fiddle with the lead reins.

Keep an eye
always on
horses.

Always keep an eye on the position of the horses, and see that they are in their right places, and that each is doing his fair share of work.

If any horse is out of his place, find out the cause, and adjust the rein or use the whip accordingly.

Grip tightly
with third and
little fingers to
prevent reins
slipping.

Always keep the left hand and elbow in their proper positions, and keep a firm grip of the reins with the third and little fingers never on any account allowing one to slip.

This cannot be too strongly insisted on, although it will be found very tiring at first, even if the horses are not pulling.

When catching or attending to the whip, beginners are very apt to drop the left hand.

Do not drop left hand.

FIG. 32.—TAKING LEADERS' REINS OUT OF LEFT HAND WITH RIGHT HAND.

This leads to horses getting out of hand, and makes them pull.

Do not allow the left hand to go moving across the body from side to side, or to move to the front to pick up the

When looping do not alter position of left hand.

reins ; except occasionally when turning to the left, when it may be useful to loop thus :—

Hold the off-side reins under little and third fingers of the right hand ; then take hold of the near-lead rein with the forefinger some three inches away from left hand ; and holding it tight bring it up as much as possible towards the body, at the same time quickly passing the left hand down so as to catch the near-lead rein in front of the right forefinger with the left thumb ; then bring the left hand back to its original position, and you have a good loop, and the wheelers are checked from rushing the corner by the lower part of the right hand pressing on the off reins.

Leader's tail over reins.

If one of the leaders gets his tail over the reins, never pull at it, but, on the contrary, slack it out. Pull the wheelers across to that side on which the offender is running ; then hit the wheeler on the opposite side, on his neck, when the movement of the wheelers to one side will probably clear the rein.

Another plan for getting the rein out is to slack it a good deal, and give the horse a sharp hit with the whip behind the pad ; this will nearly always cause him to swish his tail, when you can pull the rein quickly away.

Loosen rein fixed under tail by hitting horse.

If both the above methods fail, stop the coach at once, when a man must get down and release the rein by lifting up the leader's tail, and not by pulling the rein away from under it.

With a horse that habitually gets his tail over the reins and then kicks, it is a good plan to run the lead rein either through the throat lash, or the inside loop of the bearing rein of the wheeler which is on the opposite side of the coach to the kicking leader.

To prevent leader getting tail over a rein.

The reins can also be run through the head terrets or loops on the top of the wheelers' heads, but if this is done it is better to use a bearing-rein, because, if the horse shakes his head up and down, he will inevitably jerk the leader in the mouth.

These terrets have been almost entirely done away with, as, if the leaders pull, they put a great strain on the wheelers' heads, and if the latter throw their heads up and down to any great extent, they continually jerk the leader's mouths, whereas by passing the lead reins through the ring on the throat lash of the wheeler there is almost a straight pull from the leaders' mouths to the terrets on the pads of the wheelers.

Objection to lead reins passing through head terrets.

Side reins are sometimes useful on leaders, and have a good effect on hard-mouthed horses.

Side reins.

If on the outside, they should be fixed to

the buckle of the horse's own trace, but on the inside to that of the other horse.

A very useful kind of side rein has a brass ring sewn into one end of it instead of a buckle; a short strap or loop is passed through this ring and buckled to each side of the bit, while the other end of the rein is buckled to the inside trace of the other horse.

The ordinary rein used by the Artillery Driver on his off horse will do equally well. This consists of a long rein buckled to the outside of the bit, and a short coupling piece to the inside. If a horse pulls very hard and tries to get in front of the other horse, either of these reins will bring all the pull on to his bit and keep him in his place.

The leaders' coupling reins should not be made too long or else the horses' tails may get fixed in them—a position from which it

Fitting coupling reins.

will be found that they are extricated with difficulty. The buckles should come to within six or eight inches of the top of the leaders' tails, which allows plenty of room for taking up or letting out these reins.

To prevent buckle of coupling rein getting fixed in terret.

Have a runner fixed about a foot below the buckle on the rein, through which the coupling should be passed ; this will prevent any chance of the buckle getting through the terret. Messrs. Whippy and Steggall of London have invented another simple device to prevent this danger occurring. They place a short steel plate, about five inches long, covered with leather, and the same width as the reins, between the rein and the coupling. One end has a hole which passes through the tongue of the buckle, and the other has a runner on it, through which the coupling passes, so as to admit of this rein being altered. They also place two keepers on the rein just below the buckle. By this means the steel plate would be drawn across the terret and the buckle could not possibly get through. For the fitting of coupling reins the reader must refer to Chapter III.

In order to prevent the wheel horses from rushing too quickly round a corner, which they very often try to do, it is usual to catch hold either of both off or near-side reins with the right hand, on the opposite side to which you are turning, after having looped.

To prevent wheelers cutting corners.

When looping a wheel rein for the opposition point, take hold of the off rein from outside, but the near rein from above the two off reins.

When striking a horse be careful to keep a tight hold of him, as the whole effect of the punishment will be lost if the reins are slack or are allowed to slip.

Keep tight hold of horse's head when hitting him.

Buckles of
wheel reins
should be
close to hands.

The buckles of the wheelers' reins should be well within reach, but should not be so far up as to come into the hand when going down a steep hill or when pulling up. A foot from the hand when the horses are in draught will be found to be about right.

Cruppers
unnecessary
except with
bearing-reins.

Cruppers will be found quite unnecessary as a general rule, more especially on the leaders, but if bearing-reins are used, it is almost imperative to have them on, in order to prevent the pads being pulled forward on to the withers, and so galling the horses.

Be careful not to have any spare end of the crupper-strap hanging loose, or the lead rein will be apt to get caught in it, and give trouble. For this reason it is a good plan to have the cruppers made martingale fashion, as they have no spare ends, and only one runner is required.

Both lead and wheel reins should be Reins should
be of equal
exactly the same width and thickness, and thickness.
should on no account be short. This is
extremely dangerous, as they might be easily
dropped. It is much better to have them
very long, but about two or three feet of
spare rein will usually be found sufficient.

When leaders are inclined to fly away from Leaders flying
apart.
each other, or one of them hangs outwards,
the inside traces should be lapped round each
other and hooked into their own bars. This
will help to keep the horses together. It is
not a good plan, though it is sometimes done,
to fasten the leaders' bars together by a chain
as, if a horse kicks, and gets his legs fixed up
between the main bar and the others, it
becomes a very difficult matter to extricate
him.

The following spare articles should always Spare gear
should be
be carried on a coach :— carried.

Two swingle-trees—one large and one small.

Two traces—one lead and one wheel.

A jointed whip fixed up on a board. A leather bag containing a hand punch with assorted bits, and a McMahon spanner.

Brushing boots. Those made of fairly thick blanket will be found the most useful. They must be long enough to go right over the fetlock and overlap, and should be fastened round the middle with tape and be deep enough for the upper part to be folded down over the knot.

Collar-pads—several leather ones are required.

Sheepskin—a good-sized piece.

Needle and waxed thread.

A few spare straps and buckles.

A few cheek leathers.

False collars, which can either be made of

leather or nummah, often come in very handy.
The advantage of the latter material over the
former consists in its being softer, and in the
event of a gall a piece can easily be cut
out ; but, on the other hand, it requires a more
roomy collar.

If the team are pulling too hard, stop
them occasionally and alter the bits. Lower-
ing these in the horses' mouths often has a
wonderful effect. You can also tighten the
curb-chains, or put the reins lower down on
the bits. Do not pull at your horses more
than you can help, but directly you feel that
they are getting the best of you stop at once,
and if possible give them up to another
driver. If three of the team can go ten
miles an hour, and the fourth horse only
eight, keep the three back to the slow one,
for you cannot make him go up to the others
without galloping. When, however, you are

Alter bits when team pulling.

Pace should suit the slowest horse.

on a road coach, it is better to let the slow horse gallop than to lose time.

Galloping.   Galloping should not be attempted by the novice, for until he has learnt to take a good steady hold of the horses' heads it is really very dangerous, not only on account of the rapid pace, but because the coach will almost certainly be set rocking in a very uncomfortable manner, and may eventually be upset.

How to prevent coach rocking.   When a coach is found to be rocking, give the leaders a little more rein, so that their traces may place a more constant strain on the pole, which will then be steadied. Then take hold of the horses' heads and slow down gradually.

Horse's likes and dislikes.   If possible try and find out what a horse likes and dislikes so as to avoid irritating him. The sound of the horn annoys many horses terribly, and makes them pull. Sometimes this can be got over by constantly blowing the horn in the stable. Some hate the sound of the whip, so try and use it very quietly. Others dislike the sound of heavy carts rattling past them, and are in that case best placed on the near side.

To become a really good judge of pace is Judging pace. most difficult, but it is very important, and can only be learned by constant and steady practice.

To drive neatly the horses must above all things be kept going straight along the road, with the wheelers exactly behind the leaders. Always save your cattle as much as possible, and to this end never let them wobble across Team the road. In some teams this tendency to wobbling. wobble is great, and must be checked at once. This can only be done by continually watching them. One great cause of the coach Coach wobbling is the fore-carriage moving stiffly, wobbling, apply grease. owing to grit or mud having found its way in between the plates—a state of affairs which can easily be remedied by a plentiful application of grease.

Steering team
like steering
a ship.

Any such movement should be anticipated in the same manner that a good helmsman anticipates the swing of his ship, with a slight motion of the rudder, as by so doing he is never obliged to put his helm hard over. The unaccustomed hand always waits too long, till the ship has already swung, and then is obliged to use a great deal of helm—the result being that he makes his course into a series of zigzags.

In the same way a very slight pressure applied on the reins at the right time will keep the horses going perfectly straight and true, without any pulling or jerking.

Treating four
reins as if only
three.

To attain this end it is very convenient to treat the four reins as if there were only three, the two off-side reins being treated as one and

always kept together (fig. 33). Then all that
is necessary is to place the third and fourth
fingers on the off-side reins, and the middle
finger on the near leader to check the ten-

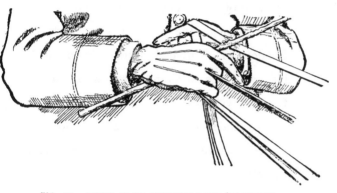

FIG. 33.—RIGHT HAND ASSISTING LEFT (ON THREE
REINS ONLY).

dency of the leaders to run to the right or of
the wheelers to the left, or else the middle
finger on the near wheeler (fig. 33), to check
the tendency of the leaders to run to the left
or the wheelers to the right. This cannot be
too strongly impressed on the reader, as the

right hand has to be more frequently used in this way than in any other.

Watching an omnibus driver is a good lesson.

A very good and inexpensive lesson in driving may be obtained by riding on the box seat of an omnibus by the side of a good driver through the most crowded parts of London. The driver has not only to gauge his own pace accurately, but also that of the other vehicles he is meeting and passing.

This renders it absolutely necessary for him to keep his eyes looking well to the front and not always rivetted on the horses, otherwise

Judging pace of other carriages.

he will be unable to judge exactly the relative positions of his own and the other vehicles on the road, all of which, at any given moment, will most probably be moving at different rates of speed.

These things have to be calculated to a nicety and almost instantaneously, if the coachman wishes to wend his way at a steady and a fairly uniform pace through the busy traffic of crowded thoroughfares like those of the Metropolis.

When he finds that it would be impossible to get through by continuing at an even pace, he must either go faster or slow down. But in either case the change of speed should be gradual, so as to avoid any sudden jerks. Change of pace must be gradual.

To be obliged frequently to pull up with a jerk not only indicates bad driving, but causes the greatest discomfort to both passengers and horses. Many London coachmen are in the habit of treating their passengers in this way, with the result that they are perpetually jolted out of their seats and experience sensations which are both unpleasant and irritating. Pulling up with jerk, bad driving.

The reason is not far to seek—these coachmen are bad judges of pace, interval, and distance, and do not see till too late whether it is possible to get through or not. They first hit their horses to try and get through, and then at the last moment finding it impossible are obliged to pull up suddenly. With a heavy coach it is impossible to pull up at once, so that the chances are a collision will occur.

How to judge width of coach.

The width of a coach is judged as far as the driver is concerned by the leaders' bars. They are always, or they ought to be, rather wider than the pipe boxes of the wheels, so that the driver knows with the greatest certainty that wherever his bars will pass his coach will pass also, always provided that he is going straight. If he is on a curve he will have to make some allowance for his hind wheels, as their track will pass a little inside that of the fore.

In passing give room to other carriages.

When passing a carriage do not move across the road more than is necessary, but at

the same time, once having overtaken it, do
not pull across its front until well clear, unless
compelled .o do so. It is considered bad
form to oblige another driver to slow down
unnecessarily. Begin to cross in plenty of
time, so as to make the incline as gradual
as possible, and thus avoid pulling at the
horses. It is far better and safer for the
beginner to give himself plenty of room,
and to slow down at once if he is not
certain of getting through. Nothing should
be left to chance.

Always take a pull at the horses to steady
them just before you arrive at the crest of a
hill, and begin to descend the other side
slowly. The pace can always be increased,
but it is most difficult to check it if you find
that you have too much way on.

Take a pull
before going
down hill.

In crossing over a bridge, like the ordinary
canal bridge, where the rise and fall of the

road are very sharp, be careful the leaders are out of draught, otherwise the jerk on the pole might cause it to snap.

The break. As regards the break, the driver should put it on and take it off himself, as no one else can tell the exact moment when it is required or when it can be dispensed with; but with the beginner, who probably has quite as much as he can do to manage the reins, it is advisable to have assistance. It should be put on, as a rule, before the coach is actually on the incline, and, if another hill has to be ascended immediately, it should be taken off before actually arriving at the bottom, in order to take advantage of the way on the coach to assist in mounting the opposite ascent.

Coming off racecourse. When coming off a racecourse with a heavy load never pull up if it can possibly be avoided, but keep moving at any price, however slowly, the wheels will then never have time to sink deeply into the ground. When this happens with a team that is inclined to jib, it is long odds against getting started again without a considerable loss of time.

When coming on to slippery stones or asphalt the horses will require holding rather more firmly than before, and it is advisable to slow down a little when approaching a corner, otherwise the wheelers are liable to slip up in turning it.

On slippery stones or asphalt.

If, while going down a hill, and especially when near the bottom, you find a wheeler slipping on to his hocks, do not try to pull him up, but drop your hand and allow the team to go a trifle faster.

Wheeler slipping going down hill.

It is a good plan for the novice to accustom himself to place his right hand on the reins when passing anything on the road, or any

Place right hand on reins passing startling objects.

object by the side of it, which might startle
the horses, so as to be ready to check them at
once should they show any tendency to shy
in either direction.

Naturally the beginner will find that it
takes some little time for his right hand to
get into the habit of instinctively seizing the
proper reins when a sudden emergency arises,
and accidents occur so very quickly that I
think these precautions may save him from
many a mishap. *Experientia docet.*

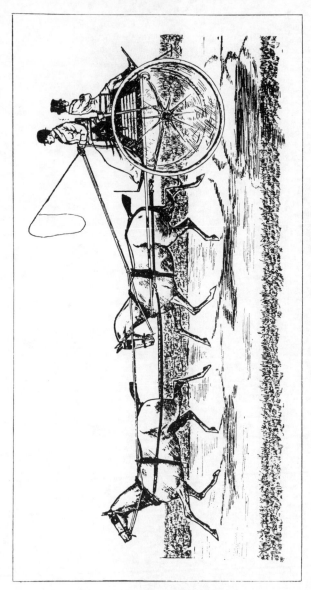

FIG. 34.—TANDEM WITHOUT BARS.

CHAPTER X.

TANDEM DRIVING.

THE fundamental principles of tandem driving are very naturally almost the same as those of driving a coach. But the chief difference between the two styles arises from the fact that both horses in a tandem turn much more quickly and with far less pressure on the reins, more especially the leader, than the pair of horses, either wheel or lead, in a coach. Furthermore, the tendency to wobble about the road is much greater, necessitating a much more frequent use of the right hand ; so that it really requires greater quickness and lighter hands to drive a tandem than a coach. On the other hand, a tandem can turn on its own

Principles of tandem driving.

Great nicety and quickness required.

ground and everything is in front of the driver, whereas a coach requires a large space to turn in, and often a good allowance has to be made for the hind wheels.

Advantages of tandem.
One of the greatest recommendations of a tandem is that it is well within the reach of many who cannot afford a team. The small extra expense and trouble which the leader entails are fully compensated for by the extra enjoyment which everyone feels when driving behind a perfect and well-appointed tandem.

It is quite a mistake to suppose that a tandem is necessarily a very dangerous turn-out to sit behind. It is nothing of the sort, if driven by an experienced coachman and the horses are fairly trained.
Idea of tandem being dangerous is erroneous.

Of course horses that have never been driven in single harness cannot be safe in a tandem. But almost every horse that will go in single harness, and some that will not,
Almost any horse will go in tandem.

will make perfectly safe leaders with very little teaching. It must be thoroughly understood that there is an immense difference between the terms a perfectly safe leader and a perfect leader. A horse may be a perfectly quiet animal, which will not kick, nor do anything that will get one into difficulties or danger, but yet be a terrible slug. This would altogether prevent one driving him rapidly through traffic ; therefore, though a perfectly safe animal, he is not a perfect leader. As mentioned above, it is necessary to use the right hand very frequently when driving a tandem, in order to immediately check every tendency the leader may have to cross the road or to turn round a corner. But if by any chance the leader has got well on the turn before you are able to check him, do not then try and do so, but apply the principle of " Follow my leader " at once. Follow

Frequent use of right hand necessary.

Follow leader if he turns suddenly.

after him, and when the horses are straight turn round and come back again. Do just the same if you are standing still, and the leader suddenly comes right round. Whilst turning the wheeler, back him if possible, so as to give the leader plenty of room. By this means you will never get the leader tied in an inextricable knot.

If it is not possible to follow the leader round, hit him on the side of the head with the whip, which will probably induce him to get back into his place.

Position of left hand and method of holding reins.

The left hand should be held in the same position as when driving four horses, and the reins held in precisely the same way, but as these matters have been thoroughly discussed in a previous chapter it is unnecessary to go into them again here.

Position of right hand when on reins.

The right hand ought to be placed on the reins in front of the left, with the

little and third fingers together over the two
off-side reins, the middle finger over the
near-wheel, and the first finger over the
near-lead (fig. 35) ; all the reins will then

FIG. 35.—TANDEM—POSITION OF RIGHT HAND ON
REINS.

be under the immediate control of the right
hand.

The two off-side reins should in all cases,
except for a sharp back turn to the right,
be treated as one rein, and always kept under

the little and third fingers of the right hand.

This, which may be termed the three-rein principle, will be found to simplify matters very
considerably, owing to there being practically
only three reins to think about instead of four.

The beginner will experience considerable
difficulty at first in passing his right hand
quickly on and through the reins in the
proper manner, the reason being that they
are all close together, much more so than
with four horses, so that he is obliged
to stretch the right hand much further
forward in order to get it in between them.
For this reason, carry your hand well out to
the front, where the reins open out a little, and
when once you have hold of them correctly
slide it back towards the body. It looks very
awkward to drive with the right hand held
out a long way from the left, and it is
also quite unnecessary.

For those who have not much expe- Always keep
right hand on
rience, it is far better to keep the right hand reins at night.
always on the reins, and particularly so at
night, when the hand should never be taken
away unless it is required for the purpose
of using the whip. Rarely pull one rein
singly, as described for pointing the leaders
in a coach, except when looping a lead
rein in order to turn a sharp corner, or to
execute a quick bend to get through traffic.
If you pull a rein singly, especially a lead
rein, you are very likely to overdo it or
jerk it.

Never jerk a rein at all except in an emer- Never pull
rein as if
gency, but apply the pressure steadily and ringing a bell.
gradually. The only excuse for " ringing the
bell " with a rein is when driving a slug which
is not going quite up to his bit, when you
want to turn a corner.

It is generally advisable, whenever pos-

sible, to advance a few paces before turning round in a road from the halt. The
best methods of avoiding any jerking when
going round corners with free-going horses
are as follows :—

Turning to the left. To turn to the left, slide the right hand
slightly to the front and catch hold of the near-
lead rein with the forefinger, and then bring
the right hand back towards the left, allowing
the other fingers to slide over, but not to
move away from their proper reins. The
near-lead rein will then be looped under
the first finger (fig. 36). When the leader is
turning nicely round the corner, tighten the
little and third fingers on the off-side reins,
and apply as much pressure as is necessary by
turning the wrist away from the body ; thus
bringing the little finger closer to it. This will
have the effect of checking any tendency of
the leader to turn too fast, while also prevent-

ing the wheeler from following round too
quickly after him, and cutting the corner.

If the wheeler is still turning too fast, drop
the left hand towards the right, which will

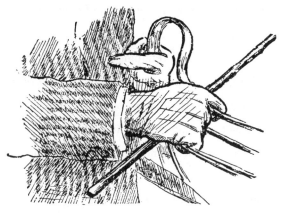

FIG. 36.—TANDEM—TURNING TO THE LEFT.

slack the near-wheel rein and so keep him off
to the right, or away from the corner. Should
the leader not turn quickly enough, seize the
loop which is held by the forefinger of the
right hand with the left thumb, retaining it
there in the same manner as previously

described for " pointing " a rein.   Another loop
can then be taken up as before, which will
bring the leader round as fast as is desired.

Best method
of turning to
right.

To turn to the right, slide the right hand to
the front, and with the middle finger seize the
near-wheel rein ; draw the hand back about an
inch or two, still retaining a grip of the near-
wheel, but sliding the fingers over the other
reins.   This is done in order to prevent the
wheeler coming round too quickly.   Then
tighten the little and third fingers on the off-
side reins, and press strongly on them (fig. 37).
This will have the effect of bringing the leader
round to the right.   If the leader is not
coming round sufficiently fast, turn the back
of the left hand down gradually, this will
enable you to turn him with the greatest
nicety.

The above methods are especially recom-
mended, as they entirely do away with the

necessity of taking the right hand out of the reins for looping purposes, the great danger of which is that it is almost impossible to get the right hand back between them quickly enough

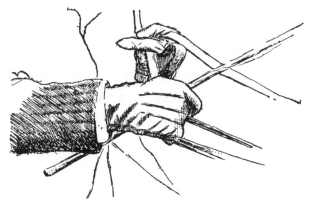

FIG. 37.—TANDEM—TURNING TO THE RIGHT.

to prevent the wheeler cutting the corner, **if** he is at all inclined to do so, or to check the leader if he is coming round too rapidly. The horses turn so quickly, that the wheeler can see the leader coming round almost before the lead rein can be seized with the left thumb, and tandem reins being very close together, it is difficult for the right hand to catch the wheeler's rein in time to check him. The fact is that several things have to be done simultaneously, or nearly so, to obtain perfection, and the manipulation of the reins is then, as I have often heard it expressed, somewhat like playing the harp. Of course with very sluggish horses the reins can be looped in the same manner as when driving four horses, but as a rule less rein must be taken up, or the leader will come round and look you in the face. Therefore you must always be ready to pull the opposite rein, and so check the horse from going too far round.

Proper time to turn leader at a corner.

Practice alone will enable one to hit off exactly the proper moment to turn the leader when a sharp corner has to be negotiated. Perhaps the best general guide is to give the leader the office when his head is abreast of the centre of the road to be turned down. More than this it is useless to say, as everything depends on the width of the road and the angle of the turn. It is, however, always a safe thing to take as much room as possible, and it is therefore a good plan before arriving at the corner to pass off to the opposite side of the road, provided the traffic will allow this to be done.

In order to turn corners nicely with the wheeler going over the same ground as the leader, and not shuffling round anyhow, or to go in and out rapidly through traffic like that of London, requires the utmost nicety and quickness of handling, and also that the horses be well trained to keep constantly up to their bits, and to feel even the lightest pressure and answer to it at once. When you drop your hand to them, they should at once increase their pace until you come back

Quickness of handling reins necessary in traffic.

Horses should answer to pressure of driver's hands at once.

to the original pressure, but the moment more than this is put on they should at once check their pace. They should also willingly go into an omnibus if driven there, and never shy off. Such is a perfect tandem, but one most difficult to find.

Tendency to slow down.

A beginner at tandem driving, and even some who have had a certain amount of practice in driving four horses, will usually find the tandem has a great tendency to slow down, and that a considerable amount of whip is required to keep the horses up to the proper pace. This tendency will be found to disappear if a practised hand takes the reins, without the aid of the whip. A want of lightness of hand is usually the cause, and a want of give and take to the horses' mouths. Probably the wrist is kept too stiff, and the pressure on the horses' mouths is as a result uneven, too much being applied at one

moment and not enough the next. To keep
an even feeling on the horses' mouths the
hand must be allowed to move backwards
and forwards a little, and there should be
plenty of play from the wrist.

When you find that the leader is going off
to the left, and the wheeler to the right, it is
usually right to push the two centre reins
back a little through the left hand from the
front with the right hand, using the whole
hand to do it with. *Effect of altering centre reins.*

If, on the contrary, the leader is bearing off
to the right, and the wheeler to the left, you
must then pull the two centre reins out a
little until they, *i.e.*, the horses, are straight.
You must remember that, although you are
using the right hand a great deal, the reins
must none the less all the time be held very
firmly in the left, and not allowed to slip in
the least ; so that at any moment you should *Reins must be held firmly.*

be able to take the right hand off the reins and the horses should still be going exactly one behind the other, with all the reins tight, the left wrist turned in towards the body with the back of the hand to the front and almost perpendicular.

This position of the left hand is of great importance, as by turning the back down or up respectively a great deal can be done in the way of directing the leader to the right or left without any assistance from the right hand. The thumb should be nearly parallel to the front, and like the first finger should be ready at any time to take up and hold a loop of either lead rein; therefore these fingers should never be busy gripping the reins. The whole four reins should be held firmly in position by the grip of the third and little finger, slightly assisted by the middle finger.

Thumb and forefinger always ready to take up loop.

Third and fourth fingers must grip reins tightly.

To get horses, which have never been in

tandem before, exactly to follow one behind the other, requires considerable skill and patience, as it will be found that their common tendency is to get one alongside the other, the wheeler as a rule being anxious to run up alongside the leader. This tendency to form a pair must be checked at once, but without any jerking or hurried pulling at the reins.

Tendency to form a pair.

The leader should be worried as little as possible ; therefore, do not pull him across the road more than you can avoid, particularly at first, but try to make the wheeler follow him, and you will find that if they are fairly well-disposed horses they will soon fall in with the idea of following one another.

Do not worry leader.

Do not use the whip perpetually ; try and work the horses chiefly with your hands, and to a certain extent by your voice. For instance. when starting them give them the

Constant use of whip shows bad coachman.

office by slightly feeling their mouths with the reins and immediately shouting " Go on," or something to that effect, momentarily dropping your hand to them in order to avoid any jibbing while getting under way. The horses will very quickly understand this, and the use of the whip will be unnecessary.

Wheeler
should start
cart.

Remember, however, that the wheeler should start the cart ; therefore be ready to touch him with the whip, if he hangs back ; if, however, he is inclined to jib, it may be better to allow the leader to assist him.

With raw and nervous horses a good start is everything. Watch the leader carefully, and when you see him starting get the wheeler off at once by using the whip if he is not moving off at the same time. When pulling up, I think it is always a good plan to say " Whoa." They very soon learn to obey the voice, and it often comes in handy.

If a horse shies, speak to him at once and encourage him, but on no account hit him or you will confirm him in the habit. He does it nearly always from nervousness, or from defective vision, and not from devilry. A shyer will often go perfectly in the wheel of a tandem and never shy at all, but is never safe in the lead. I am also a believer in rating a horse soundly when he does wrong, and especially when you are hitting him, as the next time you rate him he will think he is going to feel the whip, and be very careful at once.

Encourage horse with voice.

Never hit a shyer.

In a dog-cart, when you have hit your leader, bring the lash back and catch it quickly with a turn round the stick by a slight jerk, or bring it straight into the fingers of your right hand by the same motion. You can then at once bring it well into the cart, and get your hand back on the reins.

Returning lash after hitting leader.

This last is a very important matter, as when the leader is hit he generally takes to pulling for a few yards, and your whip hand is much needed on the reins to steady him.

On the other hand, it is very unsafe to bring your right hand on to the reins unless the lash has been brought well into the cart, as it may easily be caught up round the axle or get under the wheel ; and, as a rule, if the wheel goes over it, it will break off at that spot next time you use it.

It is often very convenient to have the whip ready to hit the leader at a particular place or corner which he is likely to want to go round. To do this unwind the lash, and keep the point of the stick out to the right front. The lash can then fly loose and do no harm, unless the wind is blowing across from right to left.

Check pace before going down hill.

Always check the pace before reaching

the crest of a hill which you are about to descend, as when once on the downward slope this may not be possible, whereas to increase the pace is easy enough. When going down a hill it will be necessary to shorten up all four reins, either by pulling them through from behind with the thumb and forefinger (fig. 4), or by placing the right hand on the reins as before explained and sliding the left up to it (fig. 35). Sometimes it will be found necessary when going down a very steep hill to pull back the leader a little, but as a rule the mere fact of the wheeler coming out of draught to hold back the cart will necessitate the shortening of all the reins, which will bring the leader sufficiently out of his collar to prevent him pulling on the traces.

Leader out of draught down hill.

The leader's reins can be shortened either by taking out both the lead reins with the

Shortening lead reins.

right hand (fig. 32), the near lead under the first or second finger, the off lead under the little finger, and then replacing them in the left hand, or else by pushing them through from the front with the right hand in front of the left, the latter being usually far the best plan.

Leader doing too much work.

While on this subject, it may be well to remark that the novice is usually inclined to allow the leader to do a great deal too much work. The traces should never be quite taut except when going up a hill, and then the leader may be allowed to do his best. The result of allowing the leader to do all the work on the flat is that the wheeler soon learns to hang back, and thus makes his companion pull him along as well as the cart, and when this happens it is almost impossible to negotiate a sharp turn safely. From this it is evident that, when going up a hill with the

Turning while going up hill.

leader well in draught, he must be taken out of the collar before a turn is attempted, otherwise the wheeler will be forced to cut the corner.

From this chapter it will be seen, that although the general principles of driving a tandem are the same as those of driving four horses, yet there are many minor points of difference, which the man, who wishes to drive both with equal skill, must carefully study and practise.

One very notable difference, which may be pointed out again, is the greater lightness and quickness of handling necessary to guide a tandem with ease and safety through difficult places.

Tandem is therefore admirably adapted for ladies who are fond of driving, as it affords all the interest of a team, without placing any undue strain on their strength or powers of endurance, while it enables them to exercise those qualities of quickness and lightness of hands, in which as a rule they surpass men.

The whole art of driving is composed of innumerable small, though most important details, but probably no other class of driving requires so much attention to be paid to these minutiæ as Tandem.

FIG. 38.—TANDEM WITH BARS.

CHAPTER XI.

TANDEM HARNESS.

THE harness should be as simple and as light as possible, consistent with strength. The colour is a matter of taste and convenience, but perhaps for country work brown with brass mounts is the most suitable, whereas for driving in the Park black harness is almost *de rigueur*. Certainly for soldiers at home, and more especially abroad, brown is far the most useful, because it is a part of every mounted soldier's training to clean this kind of leather.

Best kind of harness simple and light.

The wheeler's harness is an ordinary single set with one or two trifling additions, none of which are absolutely necessary. These are

Wheel harness.

two brass rings or loops fixed under the trace
buckles, into which are fastened the spring
hooks of the leader's traces, and terrets on
the pad divided by a roller to separate the
reins.   For the former short pieces of leather
can be substituted, which have holes punched
in one end, through which the tongues of the
trace buckles pass, while at the other end are
sewn metal rings to take the hooks of the

Lead harness.   leader's traces.   The leader should have a
pad of rather lighter make than the wheeler,
with two fixed leather loops, one at each side,
for the traces to run through.   There must
also be a bearing-strap passing over the
horse's loins, and this should be just long
enough to keep the traces level.

Lead traces.   The traces are usually made long enough
to be fixed to the loops on the wheeler's
traces, as already described.   This is the
simplest and most economical plan, but

another method consists in having two swingle-bars, by means of which the leader's traces can be reduced to the same length as those of the wheeler.

The first of these bars, which is about two Swingle-bars. feet six inches in length, has a large hook about five inches long fixed in its front, and a light chain about one foot long attached at the back. The chain is hooked to a ring in the bottom of the wheeler's hames, and is intended to prevent the bar from falling down. At each end of the bar are two short traces about two feet long, which hook into the wheeler's trace in the same way as previously described for the long ones.

The second bar is a light swingle-tree Advantages of about two feet in length, having an eyelet swingle-bars over long to attach it to the hook of the other bar. traces.

Advocates for this system claim that it is less dangerous than the other, because neither horse can get a leg over the trace, nor can a trace wrap round the leader's quarter if he swings suddenly round to study the view in rear. The second method however entails more expense and trouble than the first, which with careful driving need rarely be the cause of accidents.

Traces hooked to shafts dangerous. The leader's traces are sometimes hooked to the points of the shafts, but as this is a most dangerous system it should never be employed.

I have seen tandem traces extemporized out of ordinary single-harness traces and pole chains, the latter bridging the gap between the wheeler's traces and the leader's. This arrangement looked very smart, but must make the lead traces too heavy.

Breast harness. Although not so smart as a collar, breast harness can be used in tandem equally as well as in single harness, and as it can be adjusted to fit any horse its use avoids the necessity of spending money on numerous collars. It also comes in very useful when a horse's shoulders have been wrung by a collar (see Chap. I.).

The length of the leader's traces should depend on the length of the horses and also on their action. They should be as short as possible, but not so short as to make the wheeler appear to be stepping on the leader. Three feet from nose to croup seems to be about the right distance when the leader is in draught.

Length of lead traces.

While on the subject of the leader's traces it may be well to point out that the best way to hook them up, when putting to or taking out the leader, is to pass the end of the trace from outside under and over itself just in front of the bearing-strap, and then fasten the hook to the ring of the hames.

Hooking up lead traces.

As regards the fastening up of the lead

How to fasten up lead reins.

reins, it is usual to take a loop in the end of the rein and pass it through the terrets of both pad and hames, so adjusting it that no spare end hangs down by itself. The loop will be about the right length if the end of the rein is brought up to the terret on the pad, the end of the loop thus made being then put through the terrets as described above.

Driving bits.   The best bits for all-round work are either the

Wheeler's bit.   Liverpool or the elbow-bits, but the wheeler's should be made with a light bar across the bottom of the cheek pieces. This prevents the wheeler from catching the lead rein under the end of the cheek piece, which constantly happens if he is inclined to shake his head about, and has the effect of pulling the leader

Bit catching in rein.   sharply to one side. It is, moreover, very difficult to get the rein free when caught in this way without getting down. I think, as a rule, it is a good plan to pass the lead reins through the loops of the bearing-rein of the wheeler, instead of through D's fixed on his head-collar or throat-lash. The loops should hang down about four inches, and be quite loose, so that the wheeler can toss his head to a considerable extent without violently jerking the leader in the mouth. It is unnecessary to pass the reins through the terrets on the hames, as bringing them straight back to those on the pad gives a better lead.

Lead reins through bearing-rein loops.

Of course, if the wheeler habitually shakes his head about very much, either up or down, or both, then a martingale and a bearing-rein must be put on, which will effectually stop his little game.

Never drive with the lead reins buckled, as, if the leader breaks either the traces, or the bar (if he has one), by kicking or falling, the reins will run through the terrets, and the horse

Lead reins never to be buckled.

can then get clear away, and a worse accident be avoided. Should the leader get his tail over a rein, a good way of getting it clear is to pull the wheeler well across to the side on which the rein is fast, and the leader rather over to the opposite side, slacking at the same time the fixed rein as much as possible. By this manœuvre the rein will often come loose. If it does not, try hitting the leader on the quarter with the whip, when he will probably swish his tail and allow the rein to drop.

Leader's tail over rein.

The whip is generally a rather lighter and shorter one than that used for four horses, though the same can perfectly well be used. The usual lengths of stick and lash are about five and ten feet respectively. As to the correct method of holding and handling it the reader must kindly refer to a former chapter, where it is fully discussed. The principles are obviously exactly the same.

Tandem whip.

FIG. 39.—LONGEING WITH LONG REINS.

CHAPTER XII.

BREAKING TO HARNESS.

IN conclusion, a few hints as to breaking a horse to harness may be useful to those who have had no experience in giving a young horse his first lessons. In the first place, it is a good plan to put the harness on in the stable, and let the horse stand with it on for a time, with his head on the pillar reins.

Accustom horse to harness in stable.

In India I found that with Australian horses, even those trained to military draught, it was absolutely necessary to accustom them to blinkers before attempting to drive them. They should be made to stand in their stables, fed and taken out to water, and exercised with blinkers on, previously to their being driven for the first time, otherwise they will almost invariably jib.

After the pupil is accustomed to his harness, he should be taken out and longed with two long reins (fig. 39), never with one only. These can be conveniently made of webbing, like a common single longeing rein, but the lead reins of a tandem will also answer the purpose. The horse should have a body roller on with two rings or loops about half way down each side, though an ordinary single-harness driving pad with the tugs on, or a saddle with the stirrup irons fixed up for loops, can be substituted. In all cases a crupper should be used.

Longeing with long reins.

It is always advisable to have a fairly loose standing martingale on the bit, which should be a large smooth snaffle, the martingale being so adjusted that it will keep the bit on

Use snaffle and martingale.

the bars of the mouth, and will not allow the horse to get his head up sufficiently high to cause the bit to press only on the corners of his lips.

It is also advisable to put on bearing-straps like those of a tandem leader, in order to keep up the reins. The long reins should be passed through the loops of the bearing-straps, then through the rings on the roller, the tugs on the pad, or the stirrup irons of the saddle, as the case may be, and then buckled on to the bit.

Bearing-straps.

The horse can now be driven about and be kept up to his bit with the whip, which the operator should always have in his hand.

Use whip when longeing.

Keep him circling with the outer rein round his quarters above his hocks. This will teach him to go collectedly, and enable the driver to keep his quarters well in towards the centre, preventing him from passing off sideways like a crab. It is impossible to attain this object with a single rein, which also would have the effect of teaching him to go on his shoulders.

Another point about having the rein against the horse's quarters is that it teaches him not to kick at the trace or breeching.

If he should very much resent having the outer rein on his hocks, begin by driving him with this rein over his back. He should not be kept circling too long on one rein, but be often changed from one side to the other. If, however, one side of his mouth is harder than the other, he should be made to turn to that side for a longer period, until he turns equally well both ways.

Do not longe too long on one rein.

When the horse has learnt to answer the rein at once, and turn equally well to both sides, he should be taught to rein back.

When this has been successfully accomplished, bring him out with his harness on and long traces like lead tandem traces.

Tell off two men to hang on to these while he is being driven about. By this means the amount of pressure can be regulated, and as only a small amount need be applied to begin with, the horse will become gradually accustomed to pulling with his shoulders. It is impossible to begin too gradually ; although some horses can be taken out of the stable and put into a break or a coach at once and will go fairly well, others will be rendered jibbers for ever by this too hurried process.

Have two m.. pulling again traces.

Jibbing taught by undue hurry.

In India a young horse is generally given his first lessons harnessed to a block of wood. The block of wood is triangular in shape, and in front of it is fixed a long splinter-bar. The horse's traces are hitched to this, and the breaker, standing on the block of wood, drives

Horse-break-ing in India.

his pupil about until he is quiet enough to be put in a cart. A short pole, with a cross-bar at the top like a parrot's perch, is fixed to the front of the block, to enable the driver to steady himself and prevent his being jolted off.

This is not at all a bad way of breaking a horse, as he cannot do much harm by kicking or plunging, and the block being very light does not teach him to jib.

The horse having been taught to pull is now quite fit to be driven in a break or cart. If possible, place him at first in a double break, with a steady old horse alongside of him, which will do all the starting by steady pulling and not by jumping into the collar. Many old break horses are quite up to watching the young one, and start accordingly.

Steady horse alongside youngster.

Never forget to have a bearing-rein on, also kneecaps and bandages.

Drive the youngster on both sides of the pole for a time, when he should be quite fit to put into a single-harness break or cart.

Accustom to both sides of pole.

Always have a rope halter on a young horse under the bridle the first few times that he is put to. If he is likely to be very violent, two halters may be put on, and you can then have a man leading him on each side.

It is far better to drive him where there is some traffic than along a deserted country road, for he will go much better if he sees other things moving about, as they will distract his attention, and keep him from playing tricks on the driver.

Take young horse among traffic.

It is advisable to have him well exercised before attempting to give him any of the above lessons.

Exercise before giving lesson.

Supposing that there is no double break available, use a strong light cart with extra strong shafts instead ; but a heavy cart with

Breaking in single cart.

no springs is bad, as it will make a rattling noise and possibly frighten the novice, while its weight may teach him to jib.

In this case put a good strong kicking-strap on, but be careful not to buckle it down too tight, or it will catch his quarters if he should canter, and perhaps induce him to kick.

The bearing-rein must be loose, but tight enough to prevent him from getting his head close in to his chest. A loose martingale may also be added if the horse has a tendency to put his head up ; fasten this to the nose-band.

Two men to assist in putting to.

Have a couple of men to hold him, and try and put him in without the shafts touching him anywhere. Hold the shafts well up, and get the horse as nearly under them as possible, and quite straight in front of the cart ; then lower them quietly and run the cart up, passing the points of the shafts through the tugs.

Next hook the traces and buckle the kicking-strap on as quickly as possible. One man should be kept standing in front of the horse and holding his head the whole time, and he should never move away until the driver is ready to start. It is a good plan at this stage to lead the horse about by the rope halter, with a man on each side ready to assist, while the driver walks with the reins in his hand on the off side of the cart He can thus guide him without getting up, while the weight which the horse has to pull to begin with is materially reduced.

Hook traces before buckling kicking-strap.

If he goes along all right, mount into the cart and drive him about, keeping a man running alongside for a little, when, if he continues to go well, the man can jump up behind. If he should be inclined to jib, have

When quiet get up into cart.

him led on at once, but do not hit him. Never let the man lead him by the rein, but invariably by the nose-band or halter. When

Turning lesson.

he has gone well for some distance on the straight, teach him to turn. Begin by turning him if possible on a very large circle. If this cannot be done, have him led round very slowly, the man pushing the outer shaft at the same time to assist him, as in turning the inner one is bound to catch him on the shoulder, when he will most probably passage off sideways or rein back and get frightened.

How to start a jibber.

With a horse that continues to jib from sheer cussedness, I have found that strapping up one leg, and making him stand still until he is tired out, will often induce him to start off perfectly quietly as soon as the leg has been released.

A rope crupper may also be tried with

good effect. This is formed by taking an inch rope about sixteen feet long and doubling it. The loop is tied by a thumb-over-hand knot, forming a crupper about two feet long. Pass the loop under the tail and bring the ends forward, one on each side ; then put a man to pull on each of these ends, and the horse will most probably move forward at once.

This system is a very useful one for getting refractory horses into a stable or -loose box. In Ireland it is a common practice to rub some gravel in a jibber's mouth, and this appears to be effective at times.

When a horse is inclined to kick on first being put in harness, he can often be prevented, if not cured, by holding, or even tying up a leg, as in the case of a jibber.

If the horse is 'ikely to be a hard puller, it is a good plan to have a Liverpool bit in his mouth, with two pairs of reins, one buckled

How to guard against pulling.

to the cheek and the other to the bar, the latter only being used to check him if he is pulling too hard.

Lessons must be continuous.

The lessons must be continued without intermission daily for some considerable time, or else it will be found that the pupil very soon forgets what he has been taught.

How to fix up reins when taking out of cart.

At the conclusion of the lesson, after getting out of the cart, place the reins over the off terret to prevent them from falling on to the ground when the horse is being led into the stable.   Take care that the spare parts, which hang down on each side of the terret, are well in front of the stop on the shaft ; otherwise, if the horse should by any chance jump to the front while the cart is

Rein catching apt to cause an accident.

being run back, the rein may get caught round the stop and give a sharp jerk to the horse's mouth, which will probably frighten him.

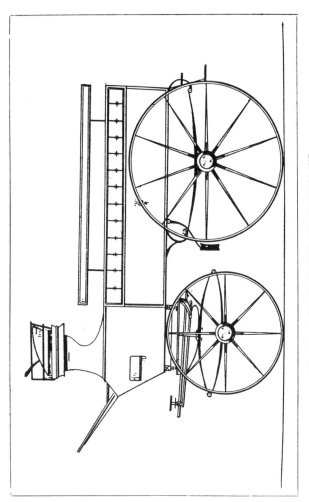

FIG. 40.—A BREAK BY HOLLAND AND HOLLAND.

Horses that have once been frightened in this way seldom forget it, and are apt to plunge forward directly they think they are clear of the traces, which is a constant source of accidents, as the horse may only get half out of the shafts, and then he will probably bolt. For this reason the kicking-strap must always be unbuckled before the traces are unhooked.

The best way of breaking a horse of this very bad habit is to drive him straight up to a wall, or into a corner where he cannot jump forward ; then unhook the traces and run the cart back.

How to prevent horse plunging forward out of shafts.

A horse that is to be driven in the lead of a team can be to some degree accustomed to the bars, by having one tied on so as to hang down and touch him just above his hocks when standing in the stable.

Accustom horse to bars in stable.

In conclusion, I would remind the reader

that " Prevention is better than cure," and in breaking a horse to harness every precaution should be taken from the very beginning of his education, for when a young horse has once been hurt or frightened, it is a very difficult thing to persuade him that the same thing may not occur again, and many a naturally quiet and generous horse is ruined for harness work, or rendered nervous for life, simply owing to carelessness or to want of ordinary precautions during his first two or three lessons.

The beginner who has mastered the foregoing pages will, I trust, find that he is thoroughly grounded in the theory and principles of driving, and his interest will, I hope, be roused to such an extent as to induce him so to turn theory into practice, that with time and perseverance he will develop into a neat and skilful whip.